Destination *Heaven*

and my journey back to life

BETH PETERSON

Destination *Heaven*

and my journey back to life

BETH PETERSON

diamondstudded treetoes, LLC
Mount Vernon, Iowa
www.diamondstuddedtreetoes.com

diamondstudded treetoes
P.O. Box 37 Mount Vernon, Iowa 52314
Copyright 2015 Beth Peterson

Publisher's Cataloging-in-Publication Data
Peterson, Beth, 1968-.
   Destination Heaven : and my journey back to life / Beth Peterson.
     pages cm
   ISBN: 978-0-9860551-5-7 (hardcover)
   1. Near-death experiences—Religious aspects—Christianity. 2. Death—Religious aspects—Christianity. 3. Heaven—Christianity. 4. Spiritual biography.   I. Title.
BT846.2
133.901—dc22

                                       2015935184

Published in the United States
First Edition 10 9 8 7 6 5 4 3 2 1
Library of Congress Cataloging-in-Publication Data
Peterson, Beth
Destination Heaven
and my journey back to life
ISBN-978-0-9860551-5-7 (original hc)
p. cm.

Printed in Canada
by Friesens Corporation

Editing by Jillian Rutledge
Book Design and Formatting by Cole Norton
Feather Art by Gene Hootman
Jacket Design by Elias Soriano
Jacket Photograph by Lisa Barta
Photograph of Beth Peterson by Sarah Werkmeister

To my Siblings:

We have survived our shattered lives.
The light has shone upon our broken roads.

Dedication

In honor of my visit to Heaven, I thank God, Jesus and the Angels above for never leaving my side and keeping my faith strong. To the men and women of our Armed Forces, their Families and to those soldiers who have served and sacrificed with their lives. To my wonderfully inspiring Grandfathers; Floyd McNelly and Jack Sharp, who both served our nation with great honor. To my husband Dave; Twenty-one years and counting. Thank you for standing beside me as I fulfill my destiny in life. To my children Angela and Casey; Keep living your passion and purpose in life and always remember, kindness rules! To Dylan Lipps; May you forever be brave and continue to inspire all of us to see the beauty in each moment of every day. I cherish your smile and the essence of faith that flows around your beautiful soul. I love you honey!

Dylan has GLUT1-Deficiency Syndrome and I would like to help bring awareness to this disease. Children with GLUT1-DS develop symptoms usually within the first year of life including seizures and various degrees of developmental delay, as well as complex movement problems. Symptoms are mild to severe seizures, developmental delay, ataxia, which is when there are not enough sugars reaching the brain, therefore starving the brain and causing all of these symptoms.

Beth Peterson

" *I never forgot my experience and shortly afterwards I began collecting other people's stories of life after life. Heaven was a real place. I gathered those stories and wrote book after book of reassuring experiences of the journey of the soul. One book became two, then three and so on.*

Imagine how delighted I was to discover Beth Peterson's own experience of a life beyond life. I was completely fascinated with her first book, 'Life after Lightning'; a book you have to read from beginning to end in one sitting!

Then the mesmerizing 'Destination Heaven', which describes her fascinating near death experience. Beth takes you with her on her extraordinary journey as she leaves this life for the next. Destination Heaven explores Beth's earthly life as she witnesses her whole life flash before her eyes, and then understands from an adult point of view, the reasons why she lived the life she did and the lessons she has learnt from them.

I've read hundreds of accounts of near death experience but Destination Heaven is the most awesome account I have ever read! Read this book and it will take away your fear of death forever. "

- Jacky Newcomb
Best-selling author of, Call me 'When you get to Heaven'
JackyNewcomb.com

Introduction

Excerpt from *Life After Lighting:*

Have you ever wondered about the purpose of your life? It is something I have pondered often. I have experienced so many different things in this lifetime, seen so many places, and met so many people. I am only left to wonder, what could be the connection of it all? The choices we make and the paths we choose all seem to have a meaning, leading us toward one ultimate purpose.

In my mind's eye, I imagine that my life path looks something like an overgrown, old growth oak tree. I have so many branches reaching outward, some paths taken and some yet to be traveled. I have been battered and bruised, twisted and cracked, hit by a couple bolts of lightning, and yet I still stand strong. My bark is weathered and my roots are never too deep. I have to keep them shallow and only deep enough to stay standing. If I were to let them grow too deep I would grow too much attachment to my surroundings, possibly not allowing myself to move on towards the next experience of my journey; the experience that my soul recognizes, that next meant to be moment on my path. So I keep myself going through the seasons and cycles of my life trying to make the connection, and ultimately, find the answer to it all.

I have loved, and I have been loved as well. I have also been abused, beyond any want of those memories. Through every victimizing experience put upon me, although I have survived, the memories still remain. I have been blessed to feel the love and light of God completely engulf me. A love that does not compare to anything in this physical life form. It was a different kind of love that encompassed me in the brightest, most spectacular light that I have ever seen. It covered me with the deepest knowing that I was not a forgotten soul, but one child of God with a connection to the other side, and to that one great spiritual being who had felt my pain. All of it. Every moment that I felt I would not be able to live through, He was feeling my pain.

I was born to be a survivor! I have had just as many victimizing experiences as I have had extraordinary ones in my lifetime; each one of them for a reason. Every one of them to give me an understanding. All of them, memories not forgotten. Why? So that I would survive to help you...

When I set out to write this book, I had one goal in mind. I had to make it a book to pay it all forward. This book is meant to inspire you to be a survivor. It's to teach you to believe in the *person that you may only dream of being. I want to show you a better way of living, not just existing in your life in a victim role. After everything I have survived, I have learned one very important thing: I am meant to do great things. For if I weren't, I would not still be alive. I would have died when I was hit by that first bolt of lightning. Now, I don't want anyone to think that their life journey has to be as astounding as mine, for each of us has a different path to walk. Each of us has a journey that is our own. We each have lessons; it is our destiny to find the answers to them and unlock the secrets of what we need to learn. I walk in my own light of knowing that I will find the answers that I seek. I have an unearthly connection to a highly spiritual belief. I am frustrated that time is wasted on self-help teachings that are full of information and seem to contain no answers and no map of direction. I wanted tools to assist me on a path to wellness; tools that I was unable to find in any book, and so I gathered them from my life journey of lessons and started sharing them with everyone around me. I quickly realized that I could talk all day but, if the words I say don't leave you with some tools to make progress, then why waste your time and my breath? My goal is to share with you the tools that I have gathered and give to you some easy ways to make yourself aware of your time, your purpose in life, and the beauty and wonder of you. I want to help you unload the baggage of unnecessary things we tend to carry around with us in life.*

My path to wellness was not an easy one to travel. In truth, it took me years to build a network of people whom I could trust to have my best interests in the forefront of their mind. In my opinion, every person seeking help should be looked at as a unique and individual human being. It is very unfortunate that we are all looked at as groups in a text book. I am my own person, different from most, and yet I have found ways to make my life, and many other people's lives, better. I find it much more healing to work on a person's past hurts, instead of medicating a person's mind where one becomes numb to the emotions they have experienced. Life is a journey of happiness and hurts. Without those hurts we would not learn the skills that we need to become better, stronger souls. We each have a purpose, a path of life events to experience.

As you set forth into this book of truth, do not feel sorry for me, for I have only endured the experiences that were meant for me to survive. Without them, I would not be able to understand, or even relate to, the painful things that you have had to face on your journey. I hope that together we can gather some of the tools needed for you to learn your lessons and really live your life.

Note to Readers

As I try to sort through my notes and memories so I can place them on this paper, something rather profound occurs to me. The memories that still remain after being hit by lightning are encapsulated into categories of survival in my mind. It's as though they have been kept in a deposit box, like very important papers for safe keeping. These memories are the proof in my own mind that I lived through these traumatic experiences. These are the things that happened to me. I survived them. As I view them I feel the emotional pain of each and every one of these life changing, mind altering, character building, and sometimes very traumatic life experiences. I ask myself if I am really ready to do this. Will the stories of what I have experienced, learned from, and survived help you in a profound enough way to make it worth me revealing and reliving these painful memories? I am left with the only heartfelt answer I can conjure in my head. It is the same answer I gave to God when I stood before Him on the other side: Yes, my pain will be worth it as I will try to help strengthen one living soul at a time and overcome their life changing traumatic experiences. It is important for me to share these things and show you that you never need to wear the victim crown. You deserve to have the tools in your hand on how to successfully survive your life journey.

My journey back to life could have been described as quite a lonely existence; coming back here and knowing the beautiful immense serenity of what I left behind on the other side. Not in a way that you would imagine being lonely, but rather in the sense that I remember what it was to be in my afterlife, to be in that glorious realm of existence. I miss the encompassing love that surrounded me so much that I have often wondered why I really agreed to come back. In all honesty, there have been moments when I wished I hadn't chosen to return.

Returning from death changes everything about a person. Reentering my life and stepping back into it, learning to readjust and relive in my human body after being out of it makes me constantly remember the weightless, safe, and enlightened place where I selflessly chose not to stay. I often yearn for the love and painless existence I was allowed to stand in, if only for a brief time. I did not return with angel wings growing out of my back, nor did I return with all the answers to my own life destiny, though I was blessed to be given the knowledge of many things to come. Most of what I came back with is far more important to those I came back to help. My death was a moment in time for me to be given a choice to be of service and inspiration to you. My return to life has more meaning now because it has made me aware of the souls I have been blessed to meet, help, or walk with on a portion of their paths. In truth, my life feels far more blessed now than ever before. In this return portion of my life I have been given an opportunity to help so many people who are in such desperate need for an answer, a confirmation, a belief in their destination and purpose of life.

As I walk you through the memories I returned with I hope to give you a clearer picture of the strength and boundless faith I have always had in my life. Had I not known suffering before, or had I not been given the knowledge of what a strong soul I am, I probably would not have agreed to return to my life here to continue this journey. More than that, I would probably not have been given the option to return. It is my faithful trust and soulful knowing which has allowed me to believe beyond any measure that I have been given a definitive path to walk.

Throughout the course of this book I will take you through some of my survived tragedies. These are the ones that were shown to me during my Life Viewing on the other side which will give you an understanding of how I have healed through trauma and pain. Without the knowledge of these experiences you would not understand the soulful outcome of faith that has carried me throughout my life journey. Some of the stories I talk about may leave you horrified and shocked, however it is important to remember I survived them. I am who I am today because of them. My desire is to help each of you heal from the derailing moments in your own lives and stand tall as you conquer the fear of dealing with them. They are a part of our life journey; they do not define us as weak. We are going to acknowledge, redefine, and most importantly, learn to forgive. For those experiences are what gave us our strength to survive this journey we call life.

When we are finished with this healing chapter in our lives we can then move on to our enlightened path ahead, our destiny path if you will. Let us start this healing process through our painful experiences together.

Almost every day someone asks me how, what, and why? Why did you get to have a choice to come back? Why did this happen to you? Why doesn't it happen to everyone? What makes you so special that God would choose you? How could you really remember what it was like to be dead? Did you really just dream it? Could you have imagined it? Is there really a Heaven? Is there really a God? How do you know for sure? Why didn't you stay there? Why did you come back? Do you wish you would have stayed? What is Heaven like?

I'll do my best to answer all of these questions in the pages ahead. Although some of the stories may be disturbing, I have to tell them in order to give you the answers. If it were truly up to me I would keep them locked away in that safe deposit box but since it is not, the story shall be told precisely as I experienced it.

Some will believe, some will doubt, and some will have their lives changed from this book. I have always been honest and very clear; this is my life and death story. I will not embellish it with glitter and gold or childhood fancy. I will share it with you just as I experienced it, as painful as it may be. It is time.

Remind yourself

to dance, to sing

to live, to love

to blaze your own trail in life.

Remind yourself

to appreciate, to accept

to believe, to become

to dream of your purpose in life.

Remind yourself

to embrace, to achieve

to encourage, to create

to persevere on your path in life.

Remind yourself

to nurture, to fulfill

to envision, to identify

to recognize when you arrive.

1

The Calm Before the Storm

It is July 20, 1992. It seems like any other Monday as I prepare myself for the workday ahead. Outside the sun is shining and it appears to be the start of a very beautiful morning, though the temperature will be scorching hot by lunch time. My shift is twenty-four hours on, then I will have forty-eight hours off. At this time I am an E-4 Specialist in the US Army serving at Ft. Benning, Georgia as part of the 608th Ordinance Company, and have finally found a profession that suits me working with a group of people who think like I do. Inspiring others in a positive way and protecting people the way I wish I would have been protected in my youth is my true passion. One could say I had broken the cycle of my own life path and the history of so many abused people before me, including a long line of amazingly strong women who, given the tools, could have broken these cycles years ago. Being a mind over matter person I have always known that I could be who and whatever I chose, as long as I set my mind to it. I have always believed that good can out-do evil and have spent most of my life proving to others that they too can survive the worst tragedies imaginable. My life could never be described as extraordinary, nor do I feel special in any way, shape, or form, however I am and always have been a very strong minded and bluntly honest person who has a tendency to reside on the extreme side of living one's purpose and passion in life. Before this day, I was simply a young woman who had survived her own life tragedies and had chosen to make a better life for herself, never willing to settle for less than was achievable. Too many years in my youth had been spent being told that I was worthless and would never amount to anything, being told I would never be good enough for the things I wanted in life. Regardless, my dreams burn deep inside and I have allowed my life to steer its own course guided by the faith I carry within me.

Today there is an extra spring in my step as I arrive at work. My smile is bigger and an awesome giddiness emanates from me. The sun shines a bit brighter and I feel so grateful for the life I am living. For the first time in a very long time my life has purpose once again. Despite this, I am bouncing back and forth between excitement and doubts about myself. It is often typical for a person who has lived through mental or physical abuse to have conflicting feelings like these. One moment you know you are exactly where you belong in life and the next a negative thought or memory can shatter the ground you just felt secure standing on. These doubts are the one thing an abused person has the hardest time letting go. By reminding myself often that one negative can crumble one thousand positives, recounting some positives confirms that I am better than the hurtful words spoken to me so long ago. For the most part I feel so at peace with where my life has taken me thus far though at times I am at odds with how I will be if I commit myself to others on a personal level. Having witnessed so many broken relationships, and having been abused in so many facets, my personal trust level for others is almost nil.

It is a bustling day at work and by the mid-morning break I have become a bit melancholy while pondering my back and forth thoughts of happiness. I had just accepted a proposal and was now engaged to be married. The ring on my finger sends waves of anxiety through me every time I allow myself to think about it and flood gates open up at random moments to fill me with doubts deeper than the Grand Canyon. The thought of finally being a part of a circle of love, finally knowing that another human being loves me back the way I love him is exhilarating. Today I am in the midst of a decision that not only affects me but also includes a child. This is one of the most incredible choices a person can make in their life. It is not just marriage to one person, but rather a lifelong commitment to another person's child as well; an absolute belief that you have something to give the child that will make a significant difference in their life, not break them down or make them feel as though they aren't a part of this new family circle. The dilemma is this: can I be a better step-parent than what I had been subjected to and burdened with? Can I be who and what this child needs me to be, unconditionally? I want a family but am unsure if I know how to be a part of one. Can I be a wife and an instant mother?

Will I be able to be good enough? Like my mother before me I have always been the fixer in past relationships. We both have a foolish inclination that we can fix someone and teach them to be a better person, though I had learned the hard way a person's kindness and love is either within them or it isn't. Having experienced so much with my mother through her relationships taught me at an early age how to see through people. You can't teach someone how to treat people better, some are just prone to their own selfish meanness. It is obvious that I lack trust in other people, however I am not sure if I trust myself to make this decision either. On my break I pray for God to reveal the answers and show me the path that He wants me to take. It is all so confusing, the elation of one moment and the feelings of inadequacy the next.

On this particular day though, there was no way of knowing that none of this pondering doubt would even matter because by late afternoon I would be trying to survive my greatest life tragedy of all. I had no idea that I would be making my own life and death decisions by dinner time and I especially had no way of knowing that I would never again be the young woman I started off being when I woke up this morning. If I did, I would have called in sick. (It's funny now, you can laugh with me!)

2

Lightning Strikes

The day is going quite well and I spend the majority of my time checking over the trucks and ammunition logs as usual. By this point nothing out of the ordinary has happened to give me any inclination that my life journey will change dramatically only hours from now. A couple of my favorite Army retirees and I are visiting with one another. We love to talk about hunting and fishing and they would often share with me old Army stories of their own. Having always felt a great connection with people older than myself I love to hear them talk about their life experiences. However, on this particular day I am in an exceptionally great mood, laughing and joking around, which makes the retirees want to tell me some of the more personal things going on with their lives and families. Even though it was not unusual for me to have deep and personal conversations with people, my recent engagement seems to have opened up a deeper connection between the retirees and myself. Our conversations have stayed with me because, despite always having been a person to whom others want to tell their most meaningful stories, it hadn't happened before this day with the old fellas. Early in the day one of them asked me how I felt about God. The question struck me as a bit odd, but I stopped and took the time to share with him a few of my chance moments where I felt God had been profoundly present in my life; beyond the simple knowing I feel day to day, but rather His super powerful presence in the moments I needed Him most. I have always known His essence surrounds us all but I have also had those divine moments of feeling the encompassing presence of His love when I've been living my worst moments. The retiree loved hearing my answer as much as I loved sharing it with him.

A few hours into the afternoon I find myself in another conversation relating to the first when another guard asks if I have been baptized. "Well yes," I explain as I have in fact been baptized not once, but three separate times. I chuckle as I tell him I was only covering all of my bases, I have always felt you could never have too much faith and God in your life! After explaining my reasoning and a brief family history to him he is able to better appreciate the reasons for my choices. Confused at first perhaps, but he did finally understand. Lutheran was the religion into which I was born and baptized. I later combined that into my life with the Catholic religion and sometime during my teen years was baptized Baptist. After spending time in Alaska and connecting to the Native American and Eskimo cultures and spirituality I realized that I had always felt a yearning to find and connect with all aspects of God. I was hungry to know everything there is to know about Him and was on a mission to connect every dot that I could find to help me see a bigger picture and ultimately help me feel closer to Him. Essentially, I was gathering every piece of Him that I could find. I never wanted to have an open space around me but rather wanted the full understanding of where I fit into this life and trust in His purpose for me. Some have said they can see the connection in my eyes as I speak of this. I know this is true, for when I talk about God in Heaven I can still see where I was standing that day.

As the day progresses and the humidity becomes unbearable. Growing up in the Pacific Northwest I never acclimated to the hot, sticky saturation of it. It brings on a sense of slow motion movement and everyone becomes slightly lethargic in their actions. As dinner time approaches the work day finally slows down. This is usually the time of day when I would leave for my one hour break, however today I can see storm clouds building ominously and darkening the sky above. I welcome the chance for rain to help dissipate some of the humidity and bring the temperatures down to a more tolerable level. It is, after all, a typical July day in the South and even though the rain never really cools the air it does make it a bit more breathable, which is a gift in itself.

As I sit at my desk doing paperwork sounds of intense thunder are echoing loudly in the distance. It seems to get even hotter as the storms are moving in, as though they are pushing as much heat as they can muster before giving even the slightest break. The skin on my arms glistens with sweat and I could feel it trickling down my back between my shoulder blades as I tried to focus on my ammunition logs. All I wanted was a clear deep breath of humidity-free air. The Army-issued cotton Battle Dress Uniform, BDUs, are sticking to my skin and are unforgiving to my motions of movement as I walk to file my papers. It was so hot I felt like I was standing next to a furnace. I hear the thunder roll again and pause to take a look outside. I was startled to see how dark and ominous it was looking. There was a green and purplish tint to the cloudy sky above and I could feel something strange in the air. It took a moment for me to catch my breath or to say anything, as I stood there staring up at the sky. It had the appearance of a violent angry monster rolling over us and was as though you could feel the wrath of it brewing above you. Suddenly, I realize everything has stopped moving. Pure silence, as if time stood still. I can feel goose bumps appear in a tingling cadence over my sweat soaked skin. The air is heavy and still with the promise of a powerful downpour. Never had I seen or felt anything like this. I was simply mesmerized by the look of the storm, as well as a little afraid. What is happening here? I turn to the other guard and ask him, "Are we having a tornado? It is so silent and still out here. Look!" At this moment the leaves on the trees start shivering, as though cold or trembling with fear. Not the branches, only the leaves. I ask again, "Are you sure this isn't a tornado warning?" Either way, there is no way I can leave for my dinner break in this. I had never seen a tornado but knew enough to not want to drive home in one. It is as though I am witnessing a clash of two worlds, like a scene in a movie. There are very violent bursts of energy going on above and I can feel them as I momentarily become lost in my curiosity and fear. All at once a thunderous clap and bolt of lightning collide. At the same instance the lightning hits the fence that surrounds the Ammunition Storage Point, spins and crackles on the razor wire. Time woke up. The trees start blowing this way and that in a terrified frenzy. It is time to call and tell my fiancé that I am indeed not leaving for my dinner break. Even though it is not storming where he is it would soon be heading that way. I walk back to the doorway, step out and question the other guard once again if we are going to have a tornado. I had never seen such wild violent storm clouds with colors dancing through them. Just then, the lightning cracks again and splits the tree that had been wildly blowing around. It is as though its branches were struggling against a prize fighter and there is no escaping the fury as a large branch splits and falls.

Abruptly, the clouds let loose with the heaviness of the rain they had been holding and water comes rushing down the entry road like a river pouring its way toward me. I am frozen, unable to move as the water touches my boots while I stand just outside the entry to our building. Above the thunder claps and lightning strikes again, the sound of the crash making me feel as though my eardrums have ruptured as I am lifted up from the ground and tossed like a weightless leaf in the wind. My body feels as though fire has ignited within in me and is burning from the inside out. For a brief second I hear a strangled scream escape my lungs with the last breath I had taken. Everything rushes past me as I land on the concrete and feel it had surely just blown my head off. My eyes are blinded by the flash of light, my ears deaf from the sound of the thunder. I am certain I have no head left attached to my body, and yet I cannot lift my arm to feel if it is still there. In that moment everything whooshes out of me and I know I am dead.

3

Death

My body lands hard on the concrete outside the guard building and a sensation of peace encompasses me as I am lifted out of the painful cocoon of my physical form. A great essence of tranquility surrounds me as my soul begins to float upward embraced by someone's strong arms wrapped around me. My body convulses below and I see that my head is still attached to my shoulders. There aren't any blown out holes, nor is my body smoking from being on fire as I felt for sure it had been. What I do know is that I feel protected and safe with whoever is holding me as I float above. I am confused of course, but definitely not afraid.

Oh, dear God. I strained forward to see better. What just happened? Have I been shot? Did something explode? I can see no fire, and watch while the other guard rushes towards me as my body lies convulsing on the ground below me. Strangely, I can feel his fear and am intensely aware that he is unsure how to save me. I feel his confusion as much as I feel my own. For a moment I am so sorry for him for having to bear witness to this event and I anguish for the sadness I know he will encounter from having watched me die. He already fears he cannot do enough to save me. I hear him yelling from farther away now to clear the ranges and order someone to get an ambulance. He screams through the radio that I had been struck by lightning and he doesn't know the CPR protocol for that situation. My heart aches for what he must be going through, his panic, fear, and inability to know how to save my life, unsure if I am already dead.

Often I have wondered if death is painful to people. Having been around those who have passed away from heart attacks, cancer, even car accidents I have questioned whether they felt pain from dying and have hoped and prayed they did not. What I can tell you now is that I only felt the initial pain from the impact to my body, and only for a remote second in time. Immediately following there is an immense feeling of peace, a soulful release of energy and light.

I realize I had seen enough for now and am turned away from the scenes below and go with the Angels into the light. I already feel everything will be alright for I know I am going home. I can now see the one who is holding me, as well as the other two who must have been behind me. I think to myself how amazing it is that three Angels have come to escort me home. Why three? Did they think I was going to argue? Not me, I am ready. Proceeding forward into the light I am amazed at the brightness and beautiful textures of color. Time and space pass effortlessly around us. Everything is moving so fast.

At that moment I am unaware as to who exactly the three Angels really are, although it did not matter. I feel supremely safe with them and I know they are protecting me as I am transitioned through the most magnificently beautiful lights I had ever seen into the invisible dimension of Heaven. I realize I am at peace; I am exactly where I belong at this moment in time. It seems as though we are moving a million miles per hour and yet it is as leisurely as a stroll in the park. The lights explode from white to every shade of the color spectrum like we are traveling through the most beautiful galaxy of stars and Northern Lights. All of the other colors melt away and I am left with the true colors of my soul light. It is time colliding with time; life colliding with death. One door closing and the door to Heaven opening in the brightest of lights ever seen. As I thought about the blinding flash of the bolt of lightning I knew it did not even compare to this place. It truly was Heaven. I do not know if it is the end or if it is really the beginning. As we stop our forward travel through the veil I find myself standing at a peaceful junction. Fog is layered low across my feet and I cannot see myself walking. Rather it is as if I am floating over the path in front of me. There are others sitting quietly on benches as they observe my arrival. A staircase that seems to ascend into the clouds appears before me. I walk toward it and start my climb, the three Angels still accompanying me. I have no idea where we are going and I do not question it. I hear music playing like nothing I had ever heard before and it's as though it is retuning the vibration of my soul, restoring the damage that had been

13

done to it over my lifetime and healing the wounds of my life on Earth. Nothing I had ever seen compared to where I am. Not in my entire life of imagination and creativity could I have ever pictured the beauty of this place. It is everything, all at once.

4

Heaven and Angles

I pause at the top of the stairs leading to what seems like nowhere, as I could see nothing except bright colorful clouds, and behold what a truly amazing sight it is. I feel my soul transcending through time and space, mist and color, from an earthly physical heaviness to an angelic feeling of weightlessness. My mind had gone blank just a moment before and had been cleared of all expectation, pain, and fearful confusion as the brightest lights erupt in color around me and I am granted an entrance to the other side of my life. All at once, I become immensely embellished with color and a heavenly glow of light surrounds me as I arrive in this place which I indeed recognize as "my home."

I take a thoughtful look back through the misty veil which separates my soul from my physical body and my life of living. One final look before the veil is closed. My body is lying on the concrete below and yet I am delightfully at peace with what I was leaving behind.

After all, my life would never have been described as anything even close to extraordinary, or so I had thought, though I really did try to make it the best I could with what I had to work with. I have always had a kind heart and I always tried to help others find a better path in life. I even thought I could change the world a time or two.

I am feeling as though the weight of my soul is being lifted from my body. It was as freeing as a bird soaring through the sky. I lift my arms outward and take an endless breath of energy into my soul. I feel myself stretch out into the full scope of who I really am. There are no bodily restrictions confining the brightness of my true self. I am free of the burdens that my physical life had weighed me down with. I am unrestricted once again to move with my thoughts as those who have passed before me start to move in closer. I feel a recognition of who they are and once were. Some show in their past physical form and others simply shine in their heavenly light, but I know without a doubt that I knew them and they still know me. I feel as though they were all waiting for this grand event on this amazingly wondrous day for my arrival. I can feel their salutations as greetings of love cascade toward me. I feel their pure faith for the moments that are coming; their true compassion for the life that has just ended. I feel their belief in me, but for what I am unsure. I had no idea how many people would greet me as I returned home. It had never been something I had thought about. I feel as though I had just collided with the most important moment of my entire life existence. I watch as the white mist and colorful essences of Heaven roll in around me. I remember how we have no color to match this down on Earth. The music is unparalleled to anything I have ever encountered and it washes over me with its sound and vibration. At this moment the only thing I know for certain is that I had indeed arrived!

I am still a bit foggy in my mindful thought process, as the transition I am in is all-encompassing. It feels somewhat intoxicating as I am visually taking it all in. The vibrations I feel are so refreshing to my spirit. I take an actual panoramic view of everything around me as people are still coming to greet me with their presence. I start to notice things as they appear out of what seems like nowhere. There is a giant book. I wonder to myself how it is not falling through the cloudy mist below when there is nothing to hold it up. As immediately as I think it, a table and easel appear to support this heavy and ancient looking tome. As I take a closer look at its very large cover I can see only one word, Life. I realize that I, too am suspended without a floor beneath me and start to wonder how I myself am not falling downward, when just as before a floor appears beneath my feet. I feel so safe. I feel immensely divine, to be exact. I am pain free and I am home. I am feeling quite glorious! What more could I ever ask for?

Out of the light, one by one, three extremely tall men come toward me. I recognize them immediately. I hadn't noticed they had left my side until now. One had held me as I hovered above my body and the three of them had accompanied me through my transition from life to Heaven. All three are dressed in very long white robes. From head to toe their gowns flow to the floor. They are the most beautiful beings I have ever had the pleasure of seeing. Their hair is long and white, shining with hints of sparkling silver. Not gray, but true silver sparkles throughout their white hair. They look so wise. Their faces have the appearance of holding all knowledge through time, as though they are the keepers of all there is to know about every person's life. Their eyes are a magnificent crystal blue, like that of a volcanic crater lake you can look down into and never see the bottom. The vision they held in their eyes seemed to go on forever. They have the kindest looking features, ancient with age but with the deepest wisdom I have ever seen. I can feel the powerful importance of who they are as I stand in their presence. They greet me with pure love, as well as a truly joyful sense of happiness for my return home. My curiosity is piqued though, for I have no memory of ever knowing them before this day. I do not recognize them as I did the others, those who had passed before me. I don't believe we have ever had the pleasure of meeting before today because surely I would remember them if I had.

As the space around me fills I become aware that we are all being gathered for something that feels very important. I notice that I am oddly standing alone. No one approaches me personally. Funny, I think as I didn't notice this before. Why are my people not moving closer to greet me? Before I could give that much thought, the men in white robes motion me to come forward. To stand in their presence was, without a doubt, a regal feeling. I have the incredible urge to throw my arms in the air and celebrate my good fortune! For whatever was going to *happen here is extremely important and I can feel the excitement rising from the others behind and around me.*

As I move into their circle facing the book, I take a closer look at everything surrounding me. I see how immensely tall these men really are, unlike anyone I had ever met. Their stature is enormous. Their robes may touch the floor and disappear into to mist but their amazingly beautiful wings do not. They move them in a soft fluid motion that nearly takes my breath away and it brings my wandering thoughts to a halt. Angels. I am standing in the realm of Heaven with Angels. I am feeling that today is my most blessed day, ever. These heavenly beings have delivered me home to this place. I am grateful and blessed.

What finally moves my attention is the barely visible, yet slight differences I notice between them. They are all wearing the long white robes, have bright blue eyes and wings more beautiful than anything I have ever seen, but they each wear a different colored corded belt around their waists. One is gold, one silver, and one burgundy red. Each have knots tied into them and descend clear down to the floor, with the only difference being the amount of knots. As I think about the reasoning for this their eyes begin to sparkle brighter at my thoughtful curiosity. I can feel that they are incredibly kind beings. Then, the first one begins to smile at me and starts to explain to me who they are and why they have brought me here.

5

Keepers of the Book of Life

Surely you can imagine by now how exited I am to be home. Here I am, standing in this glorious realm of my heavenly afterlife existence amongst Angels and it is even more beautiful than I had ever thought possible. I'm sure it is something we all at some point in time must wonder about, and I was particularly overflowing with grand excitement for it all. I wanted to sing to the heavens, Hallelujah!

With my giddy excitement contained, I am ready to begin. First, they explain to me that the knots and different colors of their belts show the order of their hierarchy of where they stand in the realm of Heaven with God. These Angels are of the highest rank within Heaven and are tasked with the most important jobs. They explain that today is a special day for all in attendance with us, precisely because their sole purpose was to escort me to Heaven and accompany me through my Life

Viewing. Hence, the book with its title, "Life." This important day will consist of my exit, my Life Viewing with discussions, and of course, my final decision.

Wow! All I can think is, "Why on Earth did I need three Guardian Angels to escort me home? Whatever did I do to warrant that?" Had I been back on Earth, I'm certain that my heart would have been pounding out of my chest with nervous anticipation of judgment. There however, I simply understand that they were chosen to be present, just as much as I was. I then wonder, "Is this how it is for everyone?" Immediately they answer, "No." Now I am feeling a little bit confused and the music starts to subside. It is time to get started.

I have no idea what to expect as the bright white lights surrounding me start to dim. The big heavy book opens itself to the beginning pages of my life. Magically, as if created from thin air, I notice that the story being told is also going to be played visually in that panoramic view all around me. In each scene it is as if I were experiencing it in real time. All who are gathered here will be present for this viewing of my life.

6

Beginnings

My story is a long one; longer than it should be for my forty-six years of life. There have been many twists and turns along my life path which carried me in so many different directions that it was hard as a child to keep up with all of the changes. These experiences will be retold just as they were shown in my life review.

I have learned to have faith, strength, and ultimate forgiveness. My faith has carried me through every bad experience and every lesson I was meant to learn. My inner strength comes from knowing I was never walking through my life alone. True forgiveness has allowed me to not live a broken and bitter life.

DESTINATION HEAVEN

7

My Life in Review

The scenes in my life book start projecting at all angles around me as if I am walking along with them at the moment they were actually taking place. My memories start to collide with the book's knowledge of each moment in time. Some of them make me smile at my happiness and others jolt my soul at the memory of the pain I was feeling at that given moment. I have had a million experiences in my life and each one connects me to the next. These experiences have shaped me into who I am from one moment to the next.

As I watch and listen to the scenes I am taken aback by the sheer love and joyful happiness I felt as a young child. From the approximate age of two I had to deal with things that even an adult would have had a hard time facing. As you will see, even having only one of these events could have been hard for any person to overcome and conquer. I really didn't understand *the connections until now as I stand here in the pure glorious wonder of it all.*

The scene of my first real childhood memory begins with me being very sick. My knee is terribly swollen from an effusion. I cannot see why, or if something in particular had happened to me to cause this. I assume that part is irrelevant to my viewing. What I can see was that I could not walk on my own. At this time I had a severe case of whooping cough. I can see the fevers, vomiting, and a cough that was so bad, even the sound startled me. I can feel before seeing that this is where a significant moment begins. I can see my father carrying me everywhere trying to help and comfort me. I can feel the worry from both my parents. I see my mother adding water to little bottles of pink powder, shaking them and trying to get me to drink the liquid so I would get better. I also can see the fear in my mom and dad's eyes. I would look up at them and see there is something deep in the recesses of their thoughts. They are worried I might die, as I have never been this sick before. My dad slept with me on piles of blankets Mom had laid out as a bed on the bathroom floor. I slept there for what appeared to be days. I thought the fevers must have made me hallucinate and imagine things because one night while lying there, I saw my first memorable Angel. She was just hovering there in the bathroom corner. She floated up above, smiling at me, singing to me songs I had never heard before. There were no words to the songs, at least no words I could understand, but I could feel their healing vibrations wash over me. She would stretch down to touch me on occasion and for a while there, I thought she was going to take me home with her, back to Heaven where I knew I belonged.

As I view this moment, we share the memory. I have never forgotten her. Her beauty and serenity has crossed my mind on so many occasions during my lifetime. She had very long and flowing golden blonde hair and incredibly beautiful green eyes. Her skin seemed so soft, I wished I could reach up to touch it. She wore a dark and light blue dress which flowed down past her feet. Her voice felt so caring as she sang above me. I believe the songs were meant to calm me but I also think they had a healing pulse to them.

I can see as the days pass I was getting better and the vibrantly clear detailed beauty of the Angel started to fade away. I knew that I didn't want to go with her right then, but I also did not want her to leave. I felt such an inner peace when she was watching over me. Eventually, she did fade away.

As I view this portion of my life I am elated to realize that she, the Angel from the bathroom, is standing here beside me once again, only this time I am in her world. She is viewing her portion of my life with me. I feel great comfort with her here, just as I did in that tiny bathroom so many years ago. She is magnificent, glorious in her heavenly glow as she envelops me with her beautiful angelic light. I feel that this day cannot get any better than this moment. What a blessing it is to be in the presence of such angelic grandness. I embrace her back and thank her for staying with me when I needed her most. I recall how many times I have thought of her over the years and am so elated to know she wasn't a part of my childhood imagination. I *have missed her. There were so many times I had wished to see her again during my life. I am truly grateful for this moment.*

8

Ladybug

My mom and dad and I were quite the adventurers. We loved to spend time exploring together in the forest and at the lake near our house. It's easy see how I thought we were going to have an amazing life.

In this scene from my Life Review it is apparent that things are moving toward my first real heartbreak. Around the age of four my parents had just separated and we moved out of the house we had shared as a family. It was so strange to not see my dad every day. My parents were my foundation, my friends, and the best people I had ever known, at least in my short amount of time on Earth. Life wasn't supposed to be this way, and I could not comprehend what was happening to our happiness. I could feel things were never going to be the same, and I did not understand why, or know what I could do to fix it.

Whenever Dad came over to visit we would walk to town together. He and I spent countless hours walking and talking and as we would go along the edge of the road I would find old paper soda cups and catch bugs in them. There were these tan and white striped ones I loved to catch which I nicknamed "Root Beer Beetle Bugs," though I would be hard pressed to pick one up today. I am not really a bug loving girl anymore. From where I was watching in Heaven I could see just how much I loved these moments with my dad. People would wave and honk at us as they passed by. I would tell my friends "we were two peas in a pod," just because I had heard some of the ladies at the bakery say that about us. In this scene from my Life Review we were standing at the edge of a pasture. There was a horse walking slowly toward me and I reached out to pet her. While she was standing next to me at the fence I gave her a hug and told her how much I wished she were mine. Her name was Ladybug and to me, she was both huge and beautiful.

On my fifth birthday Dad and I went for a walk and stopped to see Ladybug. The owner came out and saddled her up, then asked if I would like to have a ride. I can still feel the anticipation that I had at that moment. I loved that horse and now I was going to get to ride her! Giddy with childhood excitement my smile could not have been any bigger until my dad turned and said, "Happy Birthday!" Thinking the ride was my present, I was shocked when in fact it was Ladybug that was my dad's gift to me that day. He had made my second biggest wish come true when he bought Ladybug. Oh, how I loved my life! The man in the pasture showed me everything there was to know about that horse and I paid close attention, as if my life depended on it. I rode her home and kept leaning forward to hug her neck as we went along. Dad had fixed up the old shed out beside the duplex for her to have as a stall. He made sure the little fences were sturdy so she would not get out. I took really good care of her and brushed her so much I am surprised she had any hair left.

Ladybug became my companion, my confidant, and my friend. Too little to saddle her by myself I would instead wrap my legs around her back legs, hold onto her tail, and away we would go. We would wander all about like this; her just walking, me singing to her as we went along. She never allowed anyone else to ride her this way, but she and I had a special bond. Over time, I became really good at getting her bridle on alone. When I could find a spot high enough to pull myself up I would ride her bareback. Sometimes my sister, brother, and I would all get on her and ride together. Can you imagine three children, under the age of five, out exploring on a horse alone? I remember us riding clear out to the lake on that horse! We were living the dream of the Wild West, pretending to be explorers the whole way, though perhaps we were secretly looking for our father. Minus that one important missing piece, my life was not so bad. I had a horse and no one was around to tell us not to do things we weren't supposed to. What more could I ask for? After all, I no longer wanted to go back to Heaven with the Angel. However, life as we knew it was about to change again, and it was definitely not a change for the better.

9

Divorce

At that time my life had taken such a drastic turn of events to the point that another visit from the Angel or even death would have been welcome on so many of my childhood days to come. I daresay I was not wanting to walk through the memories ahead of me in my Life Review. There was still so much pain from them and I was unsure of the reasons for me to relive them in Heaven.

We moved forward into the next chapter of my Life Review and I could see we were at the point where my parents got a divorce. I had to learn what that word meant. A teacher at my school explained it and tried to reassure me that things could go back to the way they had been before, all I needed to do was pray about it. I had seen an Angel and I went to Sunday school at church so I knew there was someone to whom I could pray. Each day I prayed for God, Jesus, and the Angel to help me and make my prayers come true.

As weeks turned into months, my sister, brother and I learned to be very self-sufficient and independent children. My mother worked two jobs after my father left to go live and work in Alaska. The family life we had known was definitely over.

If we were poor before the divorce I didn't know it. I could see that I was a very happy child who loved fishing, collecting bugs, and hiking in the mountains with my parents. We picked pinecones and spent a significant amount of family time camping at the lake. I knew I loved my parents and they loved us, I just couldn't understand how they weren't in love with each other anymore. I knew that many people got divorced, but as a child I couldn't comprehend the depth of it. This was only the beginning of my confusion, as my worst nightmares were yet to come.

In my Life Review I looked at this scene of my mother and could see how beautiful she was. Indeed I loved her. My mother did the best she could with what she had to work with. Raising three children alone during those times could not have been easy for her. She made just over one dollar an hour working as a cook in two separate restaurants. We lived in a small duplex, which should have been condemned before we ever moved in as we lived in absolutely deplorable conditions. There were times when my mom would hire a babysitter to watch us, but only if she was going to be gone longer than usual. Otherwise, while she was working I would become the caretaker for my siblings. Often we would play outside in the field behind the restaurant where she worked.

I was five years old at this time and left to tend to my younger brother and sister. Our electricity would often be shut off and there would be no way to actually cook a meal. I made steel-cut oatmeal with cold water for us to eat, which was not appetizing at all. We would chew on cold, wet, uncooked oats, or would make peanut butter sandwiches, if we had the ingredients on hand.

I was so afraid of the dark I would sometimes make us a bed on the front porch so we could see the street light in the distance. The three of us would snuggle in together under the pile of blankets and pretend that we weren't afraid. There we would sleep until Mom got home from work.

As I stood in view of this segment of my life I was torn because none of it seemed unacceptable to us. We weren't aware that we weren't living a normal life. It is obvious to me now that we learned to adapt and take care of ourselves at a very early age. What crossed my mind as I watched these scenes was, why? What could really have been gained by this suffering in our young lives? During the review of my life in Heaven I felt God's answer wash over me: faith and survival. There is a reason for everything and each experience connects to the next.

Once, after the electricity was off for a significant amount of time, every bit of food in our refrigerator and freezer spoiled. When I opened the freezer door I thought I was going pass out from the smell of rotted food. The sight of maggots inside made me want to vomit. I shut the door quickly and again we ate uncooked oatmeal. We drank sugar water since we didn't have Kool-Aid to mix in and would tear the mold off the edges of bread so we could have a sandwich. Whatever could be found to eat, we ate. Hunger overrules gross and disgusting, especially in a hungry child's mind.

We had a few run-ins with people occasionally calling the police on us. Apparently someone did notice how often we were left alone, not that it made a difference back in those days, as children were frequently left unattended. They called about our mom not keeping an eye on us and the fact that we seemed to just wander around anywhere and everywhere in town walking or riding our horse.

At some point, I plotted out a plan with my siblings as it was my job to protect us; to keep us together and to stay safe. Whenever we heard sirens, any sirens at all, we would go to a preplanned meeting place. Our place to hide was down the backyard hill where there was an old growth fir tree with a hollow in the bottom of the trunk. I thought if we hid there they wouldn't be able to find us and put us in a foster home. We had been in foster homes briefly before and never wanted to go back again. While I'm sure there are plenty of good foster homes out there, unfortunately we never landed in one. The people in the homes we were sent to made us feel horrible, called us names, told us we were filthy, dirty, and smelly, and gossiped about us as if we weren't even standing in the same room. I wasn't able to tell them when we had taken a bath, nor the last time our long, matted blonde hair had been washed or brushed. I never fully comprehended that I wasn't able to take care of us the way a parent was supposed to.

One day in particular we were playing in the dirt under a huge fir tree in front of the duplex, the kind that grows its roots close to the surface. We were in our own realm of existence, occupying ourselves for hours at a time by digging at the visible roots with sticks and scraps of boards, making tunnels and tracks and pretending that our plastic horses and little cars were in a secret wonderland. Suddenly, we heard sirens out on the highway. We all jumped, hearts racing, and took off running. I had been digging with a triangular piece of scrap wood and neglected to throw it down. As I took off I tripped over one of the exposed tree roots. The forward motion of running caused me to fall face first to the ground. A sharp corner of the board I had been digging with impaled the left side of my chest when I hit the ground. The air in my lungs whooshed out of me and I lay still, afraid to move and unable to scream. The pain was a searing stab that felt as though it went straight through me. Even if I could have screamed there was no one around to hear or to come to my aid. For what felt like hours I lay in excruciating pain. My siblings did as they were instructed and hid from the sirens. I could not yet move and they could not hear my whispering cries for help. As was often the case the sirens were not even for us, and after a long time had passed my brother and sister came out from our hiding place. They thought that I had been caught by the sirens and were afraid. When they finally snuck over to the tree I was still lying on the ground. Gingerly they knelt down beside me and we all began to cry. The sight of my blood was scary for them and we knew I needed help. The only place to get help was from an elderly neighbor who had always made it clear that she did not like us and who had called the police on us many times before.

We gathered our courage, and with their help I was able to stand up and pull the board out of my chest, which turned out to be an extremely bad idea. I lifted the shirt I was wearing only to see blood and tissue protruding from the hole where the board had entered. The hole, being no longer plugged by the wood, started bleeding even harder. With no other alternative we went over and knocked on the old woman's door. Her house sat in front of our duplex about halfway down the drive toward the highway. It was not an easy walk for me being injured, bleeding, and lightheaded. We knocked and she answered the door, ready to be angry at us for pestering her, until she saw the blood running down the front of my shirt. She let me into her house, though only I was allowed to enter and was permitted to stay just one step inside her front door. As she called the police for help I turned my head to the right and saw a picture of Jesus hanging on the wall. He was kneeling at the altar stone with a glowing ray of light shining down on Him from Heaven. Through my blurred vision His light started shining outward toward me, like the Angel in the bathroom from when I was sick. At that moment I thought, "This is it, now is my time. I am finally going to die and go to Heaven." The last thing I remembered was sliding down her front door to the floor, staring as the light shining over Jesus spread outward to fully encompass me.

10

Heavenly Gifts

As I stand in view of this day, I am elated to realize that I have had two heavenly encounters by this early age in life. I witness the scene as the light of Jesus washes over me and I am abundantly aware of this light engulfing me again as I stand in Heaven now. It was not my imagination as a child, I am seeing and feeling it now! I am in true wonder at the reasons for all of this. My Life Review has confirmed it to be true. My soul is shining brighter now as I regain more clarity during this whole process. I am in awe at how I have been so abundantly blessed in my life. Not in the ways of society's wealth or monetary riches, but in the Heavenly gifts that were so purely bestowed upon me. How did I miss this? How did I ever deserve to be so blessed? It leaves me to wonder if these moments occur for everyone and if people choose to dismiss them, as they cannot believe them to be real. I knew of these memories but rarely did I ever mention them to anyone. I was never sure if they were reality or simply my childhood fancy. But here, as I stand before so many during this life viewing process, I can hear the elation in the music, as well as see the lights around me become even brighter. I know without a doubt that I had been supremely blessed in my life and I have no words to describe how truly grateful I am at this moment in time.

11

Painful Goodbyes

There were people lifting my shirt when I awoke and heard the neighbor telling the police how my mom was often absent. I didn't know where my brother and sister were, but I was being taken to the hospital without them. I started crying really hard, sobbing breaths that hurt badly. I was not crying for me, nor for the amount of pain my body was experiencing, but rather for my siblings. They would be afraid without me and I knew that I was letting them down. I didn't know where they were, or who was going to watch them, or if I was going to be in trouble for not taking better care of them. These were all frightening thoughts for me to consider and it was such a heavy burden for a five year old child to carry on her shoulders. I did not come to understand the weight until much later in my life when I realized I still carried it.

Because I had passed out I was kept at the hospital overnight. My wound was cleaned and stitched up and the nurses were very kind to me, although I could see something in their eyes that was not just compassion for my pain. I now know that it was a deeply heartfelt sadness, rarely shown to me by anyone, for the unfortunate circumstances of my young life.

From the hospital the next day I was transported to a foster home. It was there that I was able to finally see my siblings again. We hugged, cried and of course, I said I was sorry, over and over again. They had been cleaned up, and I was angry as I remembered very well the unkind way the woman at the foster home liked to be rough when she would brush through our long, matted, "rat nested" hair. The last time we were there I had wanted to scream at her and tell her to try being nicer to us. I hadn't had the courage to do it though, which made me feel even worse knowing that my sister had to endure that woman's harshness alone. It made me want to cry all over again. My brother hardly ever said much to other people, only to my sister and me. We all had a silent understanding, a special way of communicating with one another. We kept to ourselves, huddled together, waiting to see what would come next. Later that day, we heard someone talking to the foster mother at the front door. To our shocked amazement, our dad was standing there. Like a knight out of a storybook, he had come to rescue us!

Now, it is important for me to reiterate how much we loved our mother. She was often overwhelmed with her life. Having three children to support and working two jobs, just to keep a dilapidated roof over our heads, was not an easy thing back then, nor is it for those going through it today. She was barely making ends meet despite working two jobs, and she was doing the best she could for all of us.

Dad took us away from the foster home. I wish I could say that he just whisked us off to Alaska with him, but this was not to be. He tried to gain custody of us so my mom could get back on her feet. The family court judge saw it differently and gave us back to our mother. In truth, we never wanted to be with only one parent or the other. For us, we wanted our family back together. We loved both of our parents equally but for whatever reason our paths in life had to be separated at this time.

From this point in my Life Viewing I could see the love each of us carried in our hearts for our parents and each other. My afterlife view allowed me to see the complex choices that were being made by both parents in our lives. It gave me such clarity for how my own choices in life are rooted back to these early childhood experiences and I became more aware of the battles each of my parents had to conquer in both their lives, as well. It is truly astounding to see the tangled web of multiple people's life experiences culminating into one person's final choice to create change which in turn affects so many other people in the process. I could see the molding of my own opinions in life and where they became the basis for my own integrity.

We didn't live in the duplex much longer after we returned. I can only imagine someone must have demanded that we be provided better living quarters in order for Mom to keep custody of us, though that may be just my adult opinion speaking. The place likely should have been condemned before we ever set foot inside. So many changes took place in our lives at that time. Mom said she had to have Ladybug boarded at a farm, too far away for me to walk to visit her, which broke my heart. I begged her every day to take me to see her, even as we packed for our move.

I never did see Ladybug again. No matter how much I pleaded and promised to be good, to take better care of myself and my siblings, there was always an excuse. I was left to wonder what she really did with my horse, my most precious birthday gift from my father. Ladybug was the one thing that meant the world to me, at least in my young mind. I didn't think Mom ever recognized how badly losing her crushed me. I started to believe then that promises were just a way to get a child to behave and be controlled.

As I viewed this in Heaven I saw that my mom could not take her to the house in town where we were moving. She tried to get someone, anyone to take Ladybug, but no one wanted her. She was very old, needed medical care, and it was too expensive for Mom to afford farm fees. Even with what I know now I am still saddened by it all. The truth is, it was a great burden on my mom from the beginning, since she could barely afford to feed us children, not to mention a horse. I would not have understood this at my young age, yet my mother had to make a choice, one that she knew would ultimately break my heart if I were to ever find out. As I stood in Heaven I could see it broke her heart too, that she didn't like seeing the pain of my loss. We were as poor as poor could get and yet, we didn't even know it.

12

A Mother's Strength

The apartment complex we moved into was an incredible change for us, though we no longer had places to explore or lose ourselves inside our make-believe worlds. We spent our playtime on the sidewalk paths and did our best to hold our bond with one another together.

I started school in the Head-start program and loved it. Every day I would come home and share all that I had learned with my siblings. We loved pretending to be at school together. It was there that I started to realize how different I was from other children. The adults that knew my family treated me either with sadness or with shameful disgust. I had come to recognize the difference all too well and learned to categorize people for how they treated me. They judged me, a child, for circumstances over which I had no control. I knew it and felt it to the core of my soul. The way I was treated in my life shaped my heart to be a kinder person to others, without judgment of their status or circumstance.

When I observed this in Heaven, I could see how hard my mother worked every day, trying with all her strength to keep us fed, clothed, and together as a single parent family. For most of my life I idolized my father as the world's greatest dad, however from all of this I was able to see that each of them had strengths, weaknesses, and separate paths in life to walk. Neither of them was at fault or to blame independently for our circumstances. It all came down to it being my own tests, in my own life, as to how I shaped myself from what I had learned and survived from my life experiences. I have said this multiple times: I would not be who I am today without the experiences in my life which I survived. Never have I used them as a crutch to gain pity for myself, rather I have used them to help others see that they too can live their lives to help others learn to survive as well.

13

Comforting Presence

As I stand in the realm of Heaven viewing these important moments of my life, I can feel the emotion of the other people involved. I can see things from an outer perspective, as though I am looking at it through a glass window, seeing it from all angles from each person's view as the scenes of my life play out around me. I realize then that I can better understand the whole process of events. This big picture makes sense, where a moment before I had no real grasp of it, only my own shattered and angry emotions and memories from living through it. The missing pieces have finally placed themselves into my big picture. Up until this point my entire life was in the perspective of a child's mind and memory. I am seeing the dots connect a little at a time in this journey of my Life Review. From this vantage point in Heaven I am starting to get a sense of what my real existence has been about, though I also know what I am going to be seeing next. As the angelic presence of those around me gather their energies even closer, to comfort me I presume, I have a moment's sense of embarrassment and dread for what we are about to review. I can see the spectacular colors of Heaven become brighter. The foggy mist floating around the floor still mystifies my thoughts, yet comforts me at the same time as if it is a warm blanket of healing energy surrounding the foundation of my soul. It is a momentary distraction to give me time to prepare myself. As I take another steadying breath into my soul, it balances the vibration of energy running through me and prepares my mind for what I have tried so hard for so long to lock away and forget.

I am protected here and I am certainly surrounded by incredible Angels who already know all there is to know about me, as they are the keepers of my Life Book. I think I am safe to presume they are showing me these particular memories for a grander purpose, not coming from a place to pain me emotionally. I can feel that all who are viewing it are experiencing my pain along with me. I sympathize for all in attendance because I have already felt the depth of these experiences once. Through the viewing I can tell something else happening to me and I am not sure how to perceive this sensation. I suppose, I'll figure that out after this portion of my Life Review.

14

The Blue House

As I watched in Heaven, I could see my family packing our things. We moved out of the apartment as quickly as we moved in. If I had to guess we were probably evicted. It couldn't have been easy for my mom with three children in an apartment complex, there was really nowhere for us to play and just be kids. We were used to running free and exploring, doing all the things that kids did outside before we had a television to entertain us.

We moved into a house only a couple blocks away from our apartment. Throughout my life, I have always called it the "Blue House" because it is the house where my nightmares started and my moods became somberly comparable to its ugly color. Never have I forgotten the horrid picture of it in my mind.

Our transition into the Blue House went pretty well. It wasn't a bad house; in fact it was just what we needed because it had its own yard for us to play in. I attended Head-start a few days a week so I was able to be around other kids my age. It was good for me to be able to escape the reality of worry which I carried with me every day, though I still fretted over my siblings while I was gone. At the time we really thought we were rich. We once again had a yard to play in, a forest out back to explore, and we even had electricity. What more could we ask for? The one downside was that living here ended up meaning that we would see our mom even less, especially me because of school. Mom waitressed and cooked at two places and tended bar at another. We were alone or with babysitters more than ever before and I grew to hate this house. In reality, I came to hate almost everything except my parents and my siblings. I know that hate is a harsh word, but as a child I had no other word to describe my feelings for what happened to me next.

Please Note: I do not want this chapter to trigger an adverse effect on anyone who has experienced sexual abuse or molestation, as that is the direction this chapter is headed. If it is too difficult for you to read, please move ahead to the next chapter. In no way do I want to dredge up painful memories or create a sense of fear for you. God knows this is hard enough for me to write about and yet, I feel that I have to in order to show you how to fully begin the healing process. Even though I have already dealt with the damage from this experience, I still feel the anxiety at having to share these darkest secrets about my life. It has taken years for me to come to a place to be able to help others through their pain cycles from abuse. If you haven't yet found the tools to deal with yours, I do not want my experience to contribute to your pain in any way.

One cold day we had another baby sitter, only this time it was a man. We had never had a male sitter before. I have no idea how old he was, nor will I mention his name even though I have never forgotten it. Yes, I remember who you are, in case you are reading this. It is now time for me to tell my story.

This is the truth of what nearly destroyed me as a child. This is the life experience that unequivocally defined hatred in my heart and mind; an experience that has happened to so many other children just like me for far too long. This is the experience that changed the core existence of who I was as a child, a girl, a young woman, and later in life as a wife and mother. This is the horrible burden I carried with every detailed memory, until the day I died.

As I went about being a happy young girl with her whole life ahead of her, I was really quite unaware as to how disgusting and cruel people and real life could truly be. I had a deep-seated trust in people like I imagine most happy children do. I can remember being swatted by my dad only once for running out into the street. It was only to get my attention, to be aware of the danger ahead of me. Perhaps because of this lack in violence before this day I didn't at first have the instinct to be afraid of the strange looks this man was giving me. As the day progressed I went about my normal routine of taking care of my siblings while he watched the television. Yes, we finally had a TV, though I have no idea where it came from. It was kind of eerie to watch as it had a strange green glow to its rounded screen. I had grown to this point without ever having one so I was never really interested in sitting down to watch it much. As usual, we played as quietly as we could so we wouldn't disturb the sitter while he watched the television. I could feel his eyes watching me, though he was pretending that he wasn't. My mind kept telling me otherwise and I kept feeling like I was doing something wrong to make him stare at me, even though I knew we were being well behaved and staying quiet.

In the early evening I felt I just needed to leave the room and I wanted him to stop staring at me and so decided it was time to fix our plates for dinner. Mom had cooked hamburger casserole for us before she left and I dished some up for the three of us. While my sister, brother, and I sat at the table and ate he came in and remarked to no one in particular, "Wonder why the little mama didn't load me a plate." I looked at him, confused by the question, then he fixed his own bowl and sat down at the table to eat with us. Because we never had very much food his eating made me wish I had taken less so my siblings could have had more. There were no second helpings after he fixed his own plate. We cleaned up our mess and went back to the living room to continue playing. He would not let us go outside and I wasn't sure if he was afraid that we would go exploring or if he just didn't want to have to babysit us. It seemed all he wanted to do was watch TV. Watch TV and me, that is.

It had become important to us to keep ourselves clean and we had been doing a better job of it. I don't know if it was of our own volition or because of our mom, but we knew we had to keep ourselves bathed. I knew we were supposed to have our baths that night, but the strange feeling that I was experiencing told me no bathing for us tonight. I was not really sure what was happening, today I would call it my own gut instinct, but then as a child I didn't know what to make of any of it. To be honest, the way he kept looking at me made me tremble with fear.

After a little while longer of us kids playing on the living room floor we went to get our pajamas on. It was dark out, so we knew that there would be no going outside to play the rest of the night. When we came back to the living room we were told to sit down and watch TV, no more playing. We put our toys away and he made us sit right in front of the television on the floor. After a few minutes passed he called me over to the sofa. I stood there, waiting to see what he wanted. He grabbed my arm, pulled me down beside him, and told me I had to sit there. I told him that I wanted to sit on the floor with my siblings, but he simply said, "No." He told them to watch the TV, no talking and no turning around, or they would have to go to bed alone. Of course they would listen; we never wanted to go anywhere alone, especially to bed. We hated the dark, particularly in the bedroom. I don't think we even went to the bathroom alone. We were like each other's shadows. We were always there for each other and were truly inseparable during those beginning years of our lives. We had a bond that we knew could keep each other safe.

For what seemed like forever I sat there unmoving with a sick feeling in my stomach as my heart pounded in my ears, my neck, and in my chest. I kept wondering about what I had done wrong to be in trouble, which was something I always tried to avoid. My heart was beating so loudly and I wanted to run away but my legs wouldn't move. I knew there was no way that all three of us could get away together. As the minutes passed, I could feel him watching me instead of the TV, like he sensed I was going to run. He reached over and twirled his fingers through the long strands of my hair. Absolute fear ran cold through my brain at that moment and I felt queasy. What was he doing that for?

He waited a couple of minutes, then reached for a blanket after the other kids settled into watching the show he had put on TV. He pulled me over and made me lay down on the sofa, even though I didn't want to, and covered me with the blanket. I was so afraid. I knew that something bad, something really wrong, was about to happen to me. I could hardly breathe and my heart kept pounding in my throat. I could feel my heartbeat pumping against the new scar on my chest and it hurt so badly. He started squeezing, rubbing, and patting my legs, first on top of the blanket then underneath. Inch by inch he would move closer to me and lean farther over until his body was holding mine down. I tried to move away, but he shook his head, put his finger to his lips, and shushed me to be quiet. I wanted to get out of there. I knew he could sense I was going to jump up and run because he quickly put his hand and arm over my chest and face, pressing down hard. He shook his head back and forth, silently telling me no. My eyes were open widely in shock and I was terrified because by now he was pressing his body fully on top of mine. I could not move, I could not scream, and he now had us both covered with the blanket so no one could see him pushing my nightgown up and pulling my underwear down off of me. I did not have any idea why he was doing this to me. He squeezed my upper leg really hard to make me stop squirming away from him. In my mind I was screaming, asking God, "What is happening to me?!" but I could hear no answer. The only sound was my own beating heart pounding in my brain. He first started putting his fingers on and into my private parts, pinching me and pushing as he went. I became paralyzed with fear and pain. I knew this was wrong and I tried to twist away from him but he was just too heavy for me to get free. His face was close to mine and I could feel and smell his disgusting hot breath on my skin. Tears started rolling down the sides of my face. His hand was still covering my mouth so I could only breathe through my nose. I tried sucking in air as mucus built up in my nose from crying practically choking me. As my suffocated cries got worse from the pain he was inflicting on me I could hardly breathe. I continued to choke silently on my own muffled screams and saliva. My siblings must have heard because he stopped, turned his head toward them, and then asked them if they wanted to be sent to bed. Of course they didn't want to go to bed, not without me! My mind was screaming, "Let us go to bed!" Then cold panic came over me. What if they were next? What could I do to stop this from happening to all of us? What the hell was even happening to me? All at once I felt the worst burning pain that I had ever felt in my five years of life. Worse than the whooping cough, worse than the board stabbing into my chest, worse than the loss of Ladybug, and even worse than my dad leaving. I felt like my insides were tearing apart and all I could do was vomit in my throat and swallow while trying to suck air in through my nose. I was shaking my head and trying not to make him angrier so he wouldn't hurt me worse than he already was. My eyes were wide open staring at him in terror. I wanted to scream as badly as when the board stabbed into my chest, but like then no sound came out of me, not even a whimper. My mouth was covered and my chest was still being pinned down by his body. My entire body was being crushed, pinned, and now burning with that white hot pain. He kept pressing on and into me with such force that I felt as though I was being smashed and torn apart, all at the same time. I had no idea what was happening to me. My tears made no difference, not to this monster. For a moment I felt that death would be welcome. I must have been on the verge of passing out from pain and lack of oxygen because I could feel myself slipping away. I did not see Jesus or the Angel, and I felt utterly broken and alone. When he was finished with what he had wanted to do to me he tried to wipe at my tears with his other hand. He then leaned his face closer and harshly whispered to me that this was our secret and that I would get in really big trouble if anyone ever found out. As he squeezed my face tightly and asked me if I understood, all I could see was the crazy look in his eyes and heard the roaring sound of the TV blaring as it cast its ugly green glow about the room. I twisted my head away toward the strange rounded shape of that TV and again he breathed his disgusting breath onto my face. My eyes were flooded with tears and I could see nothing clearly. My blood was roaring through my body making a terrible screeching sound in my ears. At that moment my mind shattered like glass hitting the floor in slow motion and scattering into a thousand pieces. Every minute, part of me felt far sicker beyond my own understanding. Oh my God, I wanted to throw up.

After what seemed like forever, longer than when I laid on the ground bleeding from my chest, he finally got off of me. It hurt to breathe and I was afraid to move because of the burning wet pain. Every part of my mind and body felt a pain that I did not recognize or understand. I knew that I had to be bleeding like I had from the board in my chest. I wondered if I needed an ambulance again and should go to the hospital. When I finally managed to twist my nightgown back down my body I stood up only to feel my legs buckle underneath me. I tried again, pulling myself up by the edge of the coffee table and was eventually able to stay standing. Very painfully and walking bow-legged I managed to get myself to the bathroom and locked the door. I felt dizzy with pain from the movement. I hurt so badly inside and it burned to urinate. I looked up to the bathroom ceiling, half expecting and hoping to see the Angel. I glanced around the room looking for the light of Jesus. No one was there. For the first time in my life I truly felt like I was alone. I felt as though I had done something wrong. Suddenly, I felt a screaming rage build up inside of me and let out a shrieking war cry like nothing I had ever heard before. I dropped to the bathroom floor in tears and screamed out loud with anger. Wailing and sobbing, I pounded my tiny fists on the floor. My siblings were at the bathroom door trying to figure out what was wrong with me. I was screaming at the top of my lungs, "I hate you, I hate you, I HATE YOU!" Neither of them knew what to do, nor did they understand why I was screaming and crying so hysterically. My sister was whispering to me under the bathroom door telling me she loved me. Touching our fingers together through the crack underneath, she told me it would be alright and begged me to open the door. I couldn't move. My life felt broken. I didn't comprehend what had just happened and I didn't know how to describe it to them.

When I was finally able to sit up from the bathroom floor I opened the door and found my siblings huddled together trying to get me to tell them why I was crying. My sister whispered that he was gone. He told them to tell our mom that he had to go home early. We laid on the bathroom floor for a while, holding onto one another.

As a child I had no way of defining any of this in my own brain, let alone to my sister who was younger than me. I resorted to simple minded childhood anger. I wanted him to die, although I really didn't know what that entailed. I wanted him to walk in the street and get hit by a car because I saw that happen once on TV. I hated him. I had never really known what the word hate actually meant. The worst I could compare it to was food I didn't like and therefore said I hated. Something instinctual in me knew for certain I hated him worse than any food. I found myself hoping and praying he would never come back to the Blue House ever again. He was a monster; this I knew for a fact. He was the monster that would haunt me and my dreams for years to come.

I was eventually able to get up from the floor and find the strength to make it to our bedroom. I got us all tucked into bed together before Mom came home. The three of us were huddled together inseparably in one bed, protecting one another. We started saying our prayers out loud in unison. In Sunday school we had learned our Bible verses and loved to repeat what we had memorized. At that moment, speaking those words out loud was the only thing in my life which felt strong enough to help me live through the night. My sister kept wiping my tears and my brother held my hand tightly. With the repeated words of "The Lord is My Shepard," flowing across our lips, we eventually fell asleep.

Seeing them comfort me as I watched this on the screens around me in Heaven I knew how much we truly were meant to be together at that very moment of my lifetime. I loved them more than they have ever known.

That would be the first of many sleepless nights for me, as I was so afraid he would come back to hurt me again. I felt completely broken and like nothing I did would ever take these dirty, ugly feelings away. The worst part was that I didn't understand any of what had happened to me. I felt I had no one to tell, no one to explain it to me. The seed of fear had been planted in my brain and I was left with a massive amount of anxiety to fuel the hatred that kept building inside of me for years to come. I had no words to describe this because it was beyond my years of comprehension. Never did I want these things to happen to me again, or ever to my siblings. The avalanche of emotions that were breaking away inside of me made me afraid that I could hurt or kill anyone who ever touched me again. I didn't even understand what hurting another person was, yet somehow my mind wanted him to die for what he had done to change my existence forever. I was broken and I now knew what it was to hate someone with every ounce of my being.

If my mom noticed any of the changes in me, I couldn't tell. I was so full of hatred and anger after that day that no one could say anything to me without me snapping rudely at them. My rage was directed mostly at men, though I did not trust any other human being for a very long time.

It was no wonder I felt like that Angel up in the bathroom corner not so long ago had wanted to take me to Heaven. Maybe she already knew what was going to happen to me. I began to wish I could die, that she would come back and take me home with her to Heaven. Except, who would watch over my siblings if I died? I had so many emotions conflicting inside of my mind. I started having nightmares, scary ones of really awful things happening to all three of us. I was unable to save them; I just wasn't strong enough to slay the monster. I couldn't go to sleep without seeing his face in front of mine. I would wake up screaming and crying. Mom would come in and ask me what was wrong. "Bad dreams", I would tell her, "That's all". I could never tell her why because I was too afraid I would get into trouble like he told me, or that he would get into trouble and come back to hurt me for it. There was no way for me to win this game. He was older and he said I would get in trouble. I could only believe what he told me.

Emotionally hardened, I became a very tough girl after that and no one ever asked me why. Our summer was taken up with exploring, playing together, and spending some time with our mom. I'm not sure if she was ever aware of just how much my protectiveness over my siblings became an obsession to me. If someone tried to talk to one of them I would stand in front and speak for all three of us. It was obvious to me that anyone could be like the monster who had hurt me so I didn't allow anyone to get too close to us. My siblings were already used to me leading the way, so they never questioned my protective motherly behavior with them. "People can hurt us really badly" is the lesson I tried to teach them.

Dad had come to visit and I was so glad to see him. I didn't tell him what had happened to me, although I would have if he had asked. Sometimes I would sit there staring at him, willing him to ask me if everything was alright; ask me why I was so mean when people talked to me or why I was having such bad nightmares. He must have thought that my angry outbursts were out of character for me, or maybe he thought they were because of the divorce. I didn't like being mean to everyone. I wanted to tell him, wanted him to stay with us, protect us, or take us away with him. I wanted him and Mom to be together like it was before. I would never have lied to him, my parents had taught us to tell the truth. I trusted him. He was big and tough, he could have fought the monster for me. I would not have been in trouble if I could have told my dad, but he never asked. No one ever asked why I was so hateful.

15

Healing the Pain

As I looked back on my Life Review, I recognized how this experience could still evoke some deep sadness within me for the unbearable pain experienced through these unfortunate circumstances. However, as I watched from Heaven I was delighted to realize I no longer had any hatred or rage toward the person involved. I know my Heavenly Life View of this tragedy has truly healed my anger and hatred. This was the biggest burden I carried upon my shoulders as a child and into my adult life. God took this burden from me, and I will forever be eternally grateful.

In conclusion to this segment I will tell you this: You do not need to die or cross over to the other side in order for God to relieve you of your life tragedies or from the burdens you carry because of them. It was shown to me that He tries to release us from the pains inflicted upon us during our lifetime of living, but because we are truly able to make our own choices, He will not intercede without your request. It is then up to each of us to truly allow Him to lift these burdens from us and know it, believe it, and always trust that you are never abandoned. Indeed, I must have truly felt like He did not love me since He allowed this horrible thing to happen to me, but I can assure you this: that was not true. God is real, the kingdom of Heaven does exist, and it is up to each of us to really know deep inside our souls, without proof but with only faith to guide us throughout our life span. He really is trying to help us. Each time we ask then doubt we are giving up on the faith we claim to carry.

I want no one to feel pity for what was just disclosed. I feel no pity or shame for myself. If it were up to me, I would simply say it happened and be done with it. However, I have to share my Life Review with you precisely as it happened, otherwise I would not be being truthful as I promised Him I would be. There is a reason I was shown such specific things in my review. These are the reasons I am who I am today. They are the traumas through which I found a path of survival without losing my faith, although I readily admit I have wondered why He had allowed such devastation to occur in so many people's lives. It is a clearer picture to me now to know I have not, nor will I ever, deviate from the path I was allowed to finish walking. I am back here for specific reasons and we will discuss them further as we move along. I just want those of you reading this to know that if this has happened to you or someone you know, you too can have it lifted and allow yourself to live a blessed life. You did nothing wrong to deserve it, God was not punishing you by allowing it. You have the same choice you have always had, ask for it to be lifted from you and allow yourself to truly move on without the pain.

A memory can only give you knowledge and instinct to protect yourself from being a victim again. This goes for all injustices that cause us a traumatic experience. Whether from sexual, physical, emotional or mental abuse, a divorce, grief from the loss of someone special, anything that separates you from being able to move forward to your healing place. The pain does not need to define you and hold you down. It is your own life choice to become a survivor, just as it was another person's choice to choose you as their victim. Do not let the negative person win. Let God be the bearer of your burden and you can be victorious as you redefine yourself as the truly faithful survivor of you own life challenges. It is much easier to help another person become a survivor after you have become one yourself. Imagine the healing we could do on this Earth if we all shared this. It gives hope, peace, and strength a new meaning when we remind ourselves to trust Him without seeing proof. The proof will start showing itself in the healing.

16

Free Will

How could I feel embarrassment about something I had no control over? The feeling lasted only a brief moment. As the story you just read is played on the screens surrounding me as if it were a movie, I watch it while being protected. I am able to see it once again from all angles. Sometimes it feels as though I am actually standing on the outside of the scene while it was happening in real time. I feel like I am visiting my own life in a backward time warp. It is explained to me like this:

God did not choose this experience for me, as humans have free will to make their own decisions and choices. Sometimes we make good ones, sometimes very bad ones. God did not like nor condone the things that were put upon me as a helpless child. This is why I was reminded multiple times early in my life that God, Jesus, Angels, and Heaven really do exist. I was reminded in order to give me the confirmation I would need in my life to never doubt my faith or God's faith in me. It was so I would know strength, honor, and truth and would have the power of the light inside my soul to outshine the hatred as it tried to root itself inside my heart. Pain in one's life can harden our hearts and allow that hatred to become a black rotting wound, which can fester inside and destroy one's faith.

I never acted out my hatred for my situation, never hurt anyone else. In truth, the hate seed was planted in my heart through my own fear of this situation ever happening to me again. I used the hatred I was carrying with me and turned it around to help and protect others near me. In a sense it was my shield of protection. I taught myself at a very early age to redefine my experiences and not let them define me. In reality I was already becoming a survivor and not allowing myself to be the victim in my own painful life. I really had no idea this was how I did things until I saw it from this outside perspective during the viewing of my life. Once again, the pieces fit and I could see the future experiences that were to come and it gave me confirmation of why I did things the way I did. For certain, inside my heart I always knew where I had come from. Indeed, I knew my soul was born as a child of God. I had learned early through my lessons in church and Sunday school to always have Jesus in my heart and know he was our Savior. I always felt a deeper understanding since I had seen an Angel at such a young age and I knew there was so much more to believe in.

My energies are rising and changing color again as I am being healed from the pain subjected upon my human body and the experiences which had penetrated my emotions and wounded my soul. I am amazed at how fast the healing has changed my Heavenly light. My soul is feeling so cleansed and rejuvenated. It is as though I am almost brand new again.

17

Alaska

We weren't at the Blue House very long when we moved again. I didn't care where we went, I was just so glad to be out of there. We moved into a two-bedroom apartment, which didn't matter to us since we all slept in the same room anyway, we never wanted to be separated. We stayed in the apartment for the rest of the summer. No forest, no trees, nothing we loved to do, just the town and the complex. It was beyond boring since there was only a courtyard to play in. It was close to two of the places Mom worked though so I think it was better for all of us.

The most significant Life View shown while we lived at this place was when my mom's youngest sister came to stay with us for a while that summer. She had no way of knowing how badly I needed her, but God did. She played with us, read us stories, brushed our hair, and made us our meals. We all loved her being there. I can see how she helped me without even knowing my secret. I became less angry and I felt more loved and protected. It's funny how having a kind soul in your presence can put stitches on your invisible wounds and allow the healing process to begin. She was my bandage and my saving angel in human form, all at the same time.

The only trauma that happened for the rest of the summer was while my aunt was swinging me around in the courtyard. I felt something burn and pull in my arm but I didn't want the fun to end even though I knew I was really hurt. I didn't want anyone to be in trouble so I managed to make it through the day without mentioning it. By the next morning however, my right arm hurt so badly I could not lift it without using my other hand. I knew we had to tell my mother what happened. She took me to the doctor where I was diagnosed with a severely sprained arm. They wrapped it and I was restricted from most of our remaining summer activities. I was mad at myself because these were the best and happiest times we had had in so long and I was missing out. Our summer was ending and my aunt would have to go back home for school. It was quite heartbreaking for us. I'm not sure if she ever realized how much we had grown to love her presence in our daily lives. We certainly wished she could have lived with us forever.

When we took my aunt back home the other children stayed with her at my grandmother's house. My grandfather, who we called Papo, took my mother and me to the airport where we boarded a plane headed for Alaska. What a great surprise! I was going to go see my dad and was so excited. It was my first flight and hotel room stay, and my father took me fishing for the biggest Alaskan salmon I had ever seen. I would catch a few fish and the black bears would sneak up and steal them from my pile on the bank. My dad and mom would laugh as I cried over the bears taking my hard earned fish. My dad lived at a logging camp out of Ketchikan and their bunk house sat on floats over the water. I loved laying on my tummy looking down into the water at starfish, sea urchins, and jellyfish. I had no idea why we were there or if my mom knew how much I needed to be there, but I never wanted to leave. I had found where I belonged and yet, it was not meant to be. I was not going to be able to stay there with my dad. I wanted them to get our family back together so badly and didn't understand why it was not to be. We were having so much fun together! The week went by far too fast and before I knew it we had to fly home. That was a very hard day for me, leaving my dad there alone. I could feel how much he wanted us to stay. I had no way of knowing when I would see him again. We went back to Grandma and Papo's house and picked up my siblings. We were so happy to see each other. I told them about Dad and how sad I was to leave him. We made the long drive back home and settled in again without our aunt to keep us company.

18

Starting Anew

Shortly after my sixth birthday and the start of first grade we moved again, only this time we moved into a brand new apartment complex. I settled into a new routine: I would get myself up in the morning, get ready for school, eat breakfast, and then watch television until it was time to walk to the bus stop. I now went to school five days a week and loved my teachers and loved learning. I felt like my broken life was starting to get better. I would come home and try to teach my siblings everything I had learned. We loved to play school together and I remember how much I tried to imitate the teachers who taught me by sharing everything my mind could absorb each day.

A few incidents happened while living there, one in particular that still makes me laugh out loud today. My mom had started selling craft paints and taught us how to paint with them using her small leftover samples. One day when I got home from school I went to wake my mother and siblings from their nap, since Mom had to be at her next job in the late afternoon. My siblings had taken the paints and colored all over the sheets where she was sleeping, including the one that was covering her. It was a masterpiece composed from every color of paint she had in her kit. The fabric pieces that the samples were printed on were made out of material that resembled a sheet, so when my siblings ran out of samples they just went to painting on the bedding. When my mom woke up and saw that they had painted over and around her she was not happy! I have no idea how much that starter kit had cost her, but she was out of samples and most of her paints as well. Regardless, she held onto those sheets for years. Occasionally, she would bring them out and we would all laugh hysterically. They were a perfect set of queen sized artwork.

Sometime that fall, my mom starting dating a new boyfriend. This broke my heart and made me start wishing even harder that my dad would come back home to us. We had started going with our mom to work in the evenings which is where we met this new man. She had worked there a very long time and we were familiar with the area since we used to live behind it in the duplex. We knew all the places to play and explore. We even helped serve the customers food and coffee, not knowing that most people didn't bring their children to work. This became the normal routine for us. Mom still had to work two jobs and couldn't afford to hire a babysitter every day.

My mother continued to date this man though we kids were very skeptical of him. He was so kind to us in front of her but when she wasn't looking would give us nasty looks. When we went places together he would act happy, but would reach out and grab one of our arms really hard and squeeze for no apparent reason. Now let me say, we did need some proper guidance on manners and social skills. We did not however, need to be taught in a mean, hateful, bullying way. What we needed was attention and love, things that this man seemed to know nothing about, as we would soon find out. He was really only interested in our mother. We were just her filthy, extra baggage, heathen children, as he so frequently liked to call us. The strange thing was he never said these things in front of our mom. We could not understand why he was mean toward us even when we were being good.

As I viewed these moments from Heaven I could feel something I was never aware of as a young girl, and finally see the lost link. We were missing our father, mostly for his love and protection, as that security was lacking in our lives. It is the natural instinct of a child to feel safe in their family surroundings. We talked of our father incessantly and surely that was annoying to Mom's new boyfriend.

What a beautiful woman my mother was during this time. It became clear to me why he would want to date her. He seemed to make her smile a lot and she wanted us to behave around him. We all tried very hard but it seemed that was never good enough for him. Right from the beginning we learned to walk on eggshells when he was around. The saying that love makes people blind is true. I could see from Heaven that she really didn't notice any of his cruelty towards us. He was the kind of man who had a well-paying job and he wanted to share a good life with her, though I'm not sure if he really wanted the instant family that came with.

On Mom's days off we would go do things with him such as fishing, bowling, or playing at the lake or the river. We could always tell that he was a little uncomfortable around Mom's friends and family. We also felt he didn't like being around us. He watched us with a glaring eye and we could feel his stare burning right into us. We would stop what we were doing and turn to see that look. We were scared to death of him. He always had a way of making everybody else think that he was amazing, though unfortunately we knew different. Whenever he was out of town for work we would all relax and be our happy selves. As soon as he would return we would be like mice; quiet, sneaky, and scared of being noticed.

19

Step-Father

The next fall I turned seven. I started second grade and would walk to school alone. We were still in the apartment, which was the longest we had ever lived anywhere before. One day my siblings decided to cook oatmeal for breakfast, which is what they were used to me cooking for them. It did not turn out so well, and they proceeded to practically burn the whole interior of our apartment down. I still cannot figure out how the fire didn't burn the entire building. My mother awoke to smoke and everything in the kitchen looked like charcoal. I can still see how the kitchen ceiling had melted down in cascading streaks, like black cobwebs descending toward the floor. Everything we owned was smoke damaged but everyone got out safely. I could not believe the sight of the place, the nearly brand new apartment looked like a scene from a horror film. The reality of this fire sunk into my soul and created a new fear.

As people talked about how lucky my family was to survive it struck me that I could have lost three of the people I cared for most. In one moment in time, it could have been just me alone. My childhood anxiety heightened from these new thoughts.

Needless to say, we were definitely evicted from that apartment. Even I didn't need to be told that we had to move again.

That fire made our lives take another turn on this long winding road. We had to move in with Mom's boyfriend. I was horrified to discover that he had bought a house right next door to the Blue House. My nightmares, which had started to be less frequent, erupted inside me all over again.

If the hell that I had lived through thus far in my short life could have ended before we moved I probably would not have had enough experiences or tragedy in my life to be interesting enough to write this book. Unfortunately, my life only became more of a living hell. Where I had wanted to die before I now became focused on staying alive. It became my mission to protect my siblings, more than ever before.

The relationship started out very happily for my mom. She set out to make this a proper home for us. It was a perfect little house, white picket fence included. We all helped spruce up the place, first by adding in an unbelievable amount of flowers, painting the fence, then helping Mom plant the garden of her dreams, all while planning for a wedding that we understood nothing about.

A trip was planned and we were going to go see Grandma and Papo. Little did we know that was where Mom planned to marry her fiancé. She never asked us if we wanted her to get married, or if he was kind to us, or if we liked him. It was what it was, a life change for all of us. She seemed to be caught up in all the excitement of visiting her mother and having a wedding. We on the other hand, were becoming terrified of him. When it came to us, he just seemed angry. Something didn't sit well in our minds. We were always waiting for an adult to ask what we thought of all this and no one ever did. The ceremony was a horrible time for us. We were told to sit down, be quiet, behave, or else. Or else what? We had no idea what the whispered words, "Or else!" even meant. It was the most boring family get together we had ever attended, nothing like what we were used to when visiting Grandma's house. Mom came from a family of seven children, plus three step siblings, so we were accustomed to fun family gatherings. We were used to singing and dancing, as well as an abundance of laughter and hugs.

I should explain that my grandmother was remarried to an amazing man, Papo. He had three children of his own, so together they had ten. He loved all of her children and us grandchildren. I think she had finally found happiness in her own right. She was with my mom's real father for such a short time that she was made to get an annulment from him. Her parents did not approve of him being suited to her. She did love him, and from that love came my mom. After the forced annulment my great grandparents realized that she, my grandmother, was pregnant and insisted she get married to someone else. It was a family secret for many years. My mom had a different father than her siblings and didn't find out until the day she married my father, at the age of eighteen.

From my grandmother's second marriage she had six children. She and he divorced, and some years later she met and married this grandpa, the man that we called Papo whom we all grew to love so deeply. Papo was a protective and kind man. He had served in WWII and I could sense that he had seen and felt some painful things in his life. When I looked into his eyes, I related to him and the sorrow I saw deep within. I trusted him which, as you know by now, was not an easy thing for me to feel at this point in my life. I just had an inner knowing that he was a special kind of person.

After the wedding festivities were over we found out that we girls were going to stay at Grandma and Papo's for a longer visit. We settled in for some much needed grandparent love. We helped pick berries, learned to make freezer jam, played together, and sang songs, all without fear of getting into trouble or being hurt.

20

Grandmother's Grace

From where I stand I know once again what is coming and I shudder at the thought of having to view it. I still do not understand how so much evil exists in the living world. As I stand in this place, protected and safe, I am comforted only in knowing this fact: if I have to view my life in this way so too will all who affected my life when they pass over. Both the ones who showed the greatest love and the ones who inflicted the worst kind of pain and abuse. I am once again reminded that life is a choice of good and evil, therefore it is up to each person to freely choose which path they want to walk.

I ready myself for the next viewing and feel the energy of my grandmother who has passed before me move into my space. Her heavenly beauty encompasses my soul. She knows my pain and she knows the outcome of this portion of my life. She lived through her own sense of hell with this person and she knows that this was the day I became a savior for my sister and myself. However small I was at the time I found my courage and started breaking the ugly cycles of our lives. I am quickly comforted by her eternal love for me and I know how much she has always prayed for great strength and courage in my life. I have always loved her and I have missed her presence, comfort, and encouragement.

Standing here with her I realize it has been nine years since she passed over. I am in disbelief at the amount of earthly time that has elapsed, yet it feels like only a moment ago in Heaven's time. My ache for the loss of her dissipates and I feel the love from her beautiful aura refuel me. I can sense how proud of me she has been up to this point of my life. I am elated at being able to feel her loving essence surround me again. The loss I felt for this great lady was undeniably tragic. One moment she was there for all of us and the next, she was gone. A massive heart attack took her in an instant from us at the young earthly age of fifty-two. She was the glue that held our family together. Every person she crossed paths with felt a special connection of love and kindness from her. Her God light shined through her eyes and twinkled like the stars in the sky. I particularly loved sitting at the table and singing songs out of the old hymnal she had owned since she was a young girl. Neither of us had been blessed with a great singing voice but we never let it stop us from sharing those special moments while praising the words of God. I especially loved the holiday times when we would sing old Christmas hymns. I was so blessed to be in her presence and learn the words to her favorite songs. We would erupt with joyous laughter as we watched Papo tap his foot to our singing. I can still see the smile on his face as we have our own moments of this viewing together. We can see a glimpse through the veil and we know that Papo still misses her. He is not as broken over the loss of her anymore but I don't think you can ever stop the pain from losing your one true love. You can heal the wound and even move on in life but you can never forget your truest point of happiness, the gift in life that defined you and your purpose. I think Grandma was part of Papo's purpose in life. Papo cherished every moment spent with her. I believe he gave her every second of happiness to make up for what she had been through in her life. In so many ways I believe he was her gift from God. She died knowing that he loved her with every part of his soul and that is a rare gem to find on this journey of life. It gives you a better understanding of the meant-to-be moments when they are gifted into your life after it has been broken.

It seems funny how this side viewing has given me another refueling of energy. Each time I am in a negative I am gifted with a positive to balance out the feelings that begin. Heaven really does work in mysterious ways.

Now, it is time to move on. My next moment awaits. I am ready.

Please Note: Again, I urge you to move ahead if you have any sexually-based abuse and have not yet found the tools needed to heal. I cannot stress enough how I am not writing this for pity, only for a true account of my Life Review. There are reasons for each account and I will go over them with you at the end. For the moment though I am sharing the abuse, just as I experienced and saw it in Heaven.

21

A New Monster

After a few days we were told we had to go visit our other grandparents, the one that my Grandma had divorced. I can tell you, I still remember the strange foreboding feeling that I felt inside of me at having to be left there. This man had that same scary look in his eyes when he watched us as the one who had hurt me in the Blue House. I immediately went into protection mode for myself and my sister. Wherever I went I would grab her hand and pull her along with me. I was not going to let him hurt us. Little did I know he was good at his wicked ways. He knew better than I how to play his sick and twisted game. We tried to stay near his wife, our step-grandmother who was very kind to us, as much as we possibly could. That afternoon we were waiting to go to the booster club's Donkey Baseball game, a fundraiser where the teams played from the backs of donkeys. We were dressed in our pretty pink shorts and tank tops that our grandma had just made for us. While we sat on the stairs waiting for our step-grandmother to get herself ready something felt strange again. This grandpa demanded that we come and sit on his lap. We did not want to, but he managed to force us. We just sat there together neither of us saying a word, facing away from him, one on each leg. He made our legs straddle his and kept saying, "Have a horsey ride!" He started bouncing us up and down on his legs. I wanted to get down, to scream and run. I felt this fear building in me all over again. He was squeezing his arms around each of our bellies holding us there. I did not like to be held tightly. I wanted to punch him, to make him let us go. Suddenly, I felt his arm move and then his fingers slipping inside of my new pink shorts through the leg opening. Anger, fear, and confusion took hold over me. He was holding us there, his fingers inside our shorts, touching our private parts. I was looking at my sister who was looking back at me with a terrified expression on her face. Immediately, I let out a shrieking cry to my step-grandma. He instantly stopped bouncing us and shoved us off his lap quickly. We nearly landed on our faces just as she was coming down the stairs. I yelled again, "It's time to go!" I know he did not see that coming. I glared at him, as if daring him to ever try that again. I swear, I wanted to punch him in the face but I knew I did the only thing I was strong enough to do by crying out, even if our step-grandma didn't know we needed help. He was another monster and I was dying to get away from him.

We all got into the car and went to the baseball field. There I saw Papo's sister-in-law, my great aunt. I wanted badly to go talk to her, but I was not allowed. I didn't understand why, so I kept asking and waving at her until she finally noticed me through the crowd of people and motioned for me to come over. Thank God, somebody to save us! My sister and I rushed over to hug her and Papo's brother, our great uncle, and I immediately started whispering in her ear what had happened. With my arms wrapped around her neck, I was begging her to take us back to Papo and grandma's house. She calmed me down and walked over to my grandparents and tried to convince them to let her take us back there. They said no, this was their time to visit. My great aunt walked back over to her husband, said something to him, and together they got up and left. My heart broke. I thought they were abandoning us. Now what were we going to do?

From where I stood in Heaven I could see how I thought I may have done something wrong. Maybe they didn't believe me, maybe they were angry at me. I wanted to cry. I was unable to get the one person there that we knew to help us out of our scary situation. I had failed. How was I going to be able to keep him away from us when it got to be nighttime? I felt that bad things were going to happen, beyond what we had experienced an hour before. I didn't want what happened to me before to ever happen again, not to me or to my sister. God knows I was still trying to figure out a way to survive the memories of it from the first time. I couldn't bear to go through it ever again.

The game was over and it was time to go back to their house. I was full of dread at the thought of having to stay there for the night, when out of nowhere came the sound of a car skidding into their gravel driveway. The front door flew open and there was my Papo, mad as a hornet! He hollered for us girls to get our things and go get into his car. We hurried to do what we were told and Papo slammed the front door behind us. We rushed to the car, fearing that we might be in the worst trouble of our lives. We sat there waiting, huddled together in the backseat of Papo's car holding onto one another. We could hear yelling inside the house. A dreadful sweat washed over me. My stomach hurt and I worried I would throw up, though this fear was far less than the one I had at the thought having to stay there over night. With a strong pull the front door swung back open and out came Papo. He rushed down the front steps and into the car. I could feel his rage and wasn't sure if it was directed at me until I saw the tears well up in his soft blue eyes and fall silently down his face. He was still breathing very hard as he noticed me staring at him through the rearview mirror. Only then did I let my tears fall as well.

When we got back to Papo's house we rushed into Grandma's arms and she hugged us tightly. I knew that my great aunt had sent them to help us. I hugged my Papo and thanked him for saving us from the monster. That was the first time Papo and I had ever cried together, though it would not be the last. That day I knew he had saved our lives from more tragedy. Later on in my life he would tell other people that I saved his life in return.

22

Summer Surprise

We returned home and nothing was ever mentioned about our rescue, or what had occurred to warrant it. We never discussed it with our mom, or anyone else for that matter. I can only assume they were told what had happened to us but, as with the monster before him, I didn't bring it up. It was better left in the closet of my mind where I tried to keep the memories of them both tightly locked away.

Upon our return, everything appeared wonderful in Mom's life. She was only working one job now and seemed really happy. She liked having her own money to buy items for the house and things she was never able to have before. I think for my mom it was a kind of fairytale life. She had quit working in the restaurant business and became a door-to-door makeup salesperson in her spare time. She no longer had to work to survive which seemed to take so much pressure off of her. We got to see such a beautiful side of her. She spent her days gardening and selling makeup to all her friends. We had the best meals. Mom was an amazing cook and she loved making things fresh from her garden. From an outsider's perspective it appeared that we had become a normal family.

Our stepdad had put up a new swing set and built an amazing playhouse in the backyard, complete with a slide exiting the top floor. He seemed to be trying to be nicer to us and we were trying to be good children for him as well. Life just seemed to feel a little less heavy and we all noticed the changes. During that summer he put a big swimming pool in the backyard and we spent countless hours between there and the playhouse. This was a summer full of happy surprises, the biggest surprise being a new baby sister! She was so precious, and we all wanted to hold her constantly. She gave us a new hope for happiness in our lives. Everyone's moods seemed to brighten simply because she was born. Mom was able to stay home with us we began to know how a real family was supposed to function. Our stepdad did so many things to make my mom's life be everything she had ever wanted.

I'm sure he was trying to give us all the best life he could. I also think that in the beginning, he was only trying to teach us to be better than we were. However, somewhere on this journey the niceness wore off, just as the happiness in their marriage did. Again, we were too young to comprehend what had changed between them and why we started receiving the brunt of his anger, but we did and at times it was unbearable.

23

Lessons

As I continued my Life Review from Heaven of these happy and difficult times during my youth, it is important for me to remind you that none of these abuses define my life or my feelings toward those involved today. All of our life experiences happen for reasons sometimes unknown to us. They are lessons in a person's life which give them choices, or gain them an understanding between good and bad.

I am not condoning the punishment inflicted upon us by an adult, as we were only young children unable to understand or to defend ourselves. We lived through and survived some very unacceptable behaviors from some adults who obviously had to be impaired in some way. Still to this day I do not have the answers as to why some people lose their minds and choose to treat others with such cruelty. However, I do know that in today's world they would go to prison for this kind of behavior against a child, as these types of acts are intolerable crimes and are now taken very seriously.

24

A Different Kind of Terror

I watched the scenes of our family life change from fearful to relaxed and mostly happy. We were starting to feel less afraid and more like we were all going to be alright. It seemed that if we acted like we were expected to then everything would be good. We thought we were getting the hang of this new way of living.

A year passed with only spurts of anger in our household. Two of us were in school now and we seemed to be living in the normal realm. We had found the boundaries of where our behavior and expectation lay.

Out of nowhere, everything changed. Something between my mother and stepfather must have happened, the details of which I am still unaware today. The reasons do not belong to my story, so I am not shown the answer during my Life Viewing. Our happiness turned into a very toxic and abusive way of life. What looked like the perfect little suburban family with the white house, picket fence, and a backyard full of fun things to play on, was anything but perfect.

For a moment in my Life Review I didn't think I needed to see this since I have never been able to forget any of it. This life of physical and emotional torment is still burned into my memory today. As I saw the most poignant moments appear around me, I realized I was still confused. Why did any of this have to happen? For so much of my life I felt like I was walking on broken glass, constantly afraid of everyone and everything. I tried so hard to be quiet; I never wanted to be noticed or be the one to spark his anger and rage. I couldn't stand the pain of it.

Remember when I said I had only been swatted once and that was for going into the street? Well, this time in my life was completely different. In this chapter of my life I could do absolutely nothing right. There was never a specific reason for us to line up under the willow tree and be told to pick out a switch. If I picked a small one I would be mocked and made to get a larger one. We would get a beating for simply being alive, for breathing too loudly. I was certainly not stupid, even though I was told I was every day. I came to recognize these things would happen for no reason at all. I could laugh too loudly and set off the rage. I have said for years that I do not have a very good sense of humor today, and that's because it was beaten out of me as a child. I do not exaggerate these stories; I stood in Heaven and watched myself as a defenseless little girl against a grown man and could see the rage on his face as he swung and swung at my back, torso, bottom, and legs. It never mattered where it landed, it hurt the same everywhere. On some of the worst days we would be made to have a hot bath. The water burned the welts to such a suffering degree of pain I felt I would pass out. I was always left feeling sick and nauseated for hours, the sweat beading and burning the fresh welts.

I had never told anyone about these incidences, as we were always threatened with consequences if we did. I often wondered if all my friends lived this way, but was never brave enough to ask. I think in my heart I knew they did not and I didn't really want to know the truth.

As I watched from Heaven I could see a teacher at school walking down the row between desks. She reached out and tried to pull the bottom of my shirt down which had risen up my back. She was horrified to discover the cloth was stuck to my skin because the welts had broken open and oozed. Watching my Life Review I could see the look of fear and terror in my own eyes as I begged her not to tell. I was scared to death because I knew I would get into more trouble if she told. I took the threats seriously; when he said don't tell I knew not to. Tears filled her eyes and she turned away as they started falling down her cheeks. She dismissed the rest of the class for recess and motioned me to her desk. While I stood there she tried to gently pry my shirt away from my broken, damaged skin to see how bad it really was. My head hung down in shame. I didn't want her to think I was a bad person.

There were times I would be sitting at the dinner table when out of nowhere would come an arm across my face that knocked me and my chair clear over backwards, my head hitting the floor and my food flying. I must have chewed with my mouth open, as numerous time he smacked me in the teeth with a fist or fork for that. It didn't matter if my nose was plugged from being sick, it was never allowed. On the occasions that Mom would witness any of these events it always triggered a huge fight between them. Little did she know how often these incidences were happening.

There were other times when I would be lying on the floor watching a television program before bedtime and would receive a booted kick to my ribs or legs. Why? Perhaps I laughed at the TV. Maybe I did nothing at all. Most often it was his way of saying it was bedtime.

During these episodes I became so accustomed to pain. I mentally found a way to harden my mind against any reaction to it, which only spurred the anger and caused me to be treated worse. He would call me defiant and stupid. I found ways to lie to him and say it was me, that I did whatever was wrong and take the blame so my siblings wouldn't have to. Sometimes it worked and sometimes I would guess wrong as to why he was angry. Those times he would know I was lying and we would all receive his wrath. I could see in my Viewing that there wasn't any particular reason to why we were going to deserve such a severe form of punishment. I also became aware that he was doing this only when our mom was not there to witness it. Whenever she was gone he would threaten us and say she would be upset if she found out how bad we were. We never wanted to disappoint her, and he knew it. My Review is giving me no specific answer to this portion in my life which has haunted my memories. I have always wondered what I had really done wrong, what I did to make another person hate me badly enough to inflict this much pain.

His moods happened in cycles, he was not always angry every day. There were breaks in the madness, which made it even more difficult for me to predict. I understand now why I became the worrywart child, as I was described by many in my family. As a young girl I was incessantly nervous about everything. I had to know what to expect at every turn and often became panicked if things were out of order for my schedule.

The fact is we had learned to have no emotion or fun at all when he was around. We really were trying to be very good kids and we did try to love him. That's where the confusion came in; we never knew what triggered it. It is true that a person can be controlled through fear. Let me tell you, I would only have had to experience this pain once to fear it ever happening again. Unfortunately, it happened far too often for too many years.

In the next view I saw myself lying on my own bed, as us kids were no longer allowed to share one together. We were all still very afraid of the dark but we were not allowed to get up at night for anything once we were tucked in. This was the cause of my next issue; I became a bed wetter. I was not allowed to get up, though I was scared to death to try in any case. It was a catch twenty-two for me. I was called more names over this situation, disciplined more times than I can count for it, and was deprived of drinking fluids any time after dinner to try to get me to stop. The next solution was to tie me in a trash bag so I wouldn't ruin the bedding and furniture. I was called a disgusting heathen, stupid, and an ungrateful person for not respecting how hard he had worked to buy me the nice bed I was sleeping on. He thought all I wanted to do was ruin what he had "worked his ass off for". I was a menace and a pathetic excuse for a daughter. He would ask me, "Who would ever want to be around a person who pissed themselves every day?". I slept in those trash bags, tied all the way up around my neck, until I was twelve years old.

The strangest thing is that it wasn't until I moved to his house and had to endure this kind of mental, verbal, and physical torment, abuse and degradation that no child should ever experience, that I started wetting the bed. I had never wet the bed before, even after I had been molested. These things started because of him, yet he punished me for them for years. The good news was that I stopped after he and my mother got divorced.

These are my lessons of understanding here. It really is not the abuse I sustained from his rage (which I knew was wrong), but rather how my character was molded because of it. He controlled me through fear and degradation which caused me to fear and doubt almost everything about myself for so many years to come. He did not ever try to build my confidence and strength in life, as a parent or step-parent should. Instead, he took any confidence I ever gained away from me at every turn. His unpredictable behavior led me to be on alert constantly. I literally became physically, mentally, and emotionally controlled. I was completely powerless and had no idea that it wasn't normal, although instinctively I felt it was wrong. These learned behaviors were another cycle in my life through which I had to redefine myself from a victim to truly being a survivor.

25

Forgiveness

As I look deeper I can see the emotions of my situation and am able to see how my step-father too has an aura of pain which surrounds him. I am not sure what his reasons are because it does not belong to me, however I can see that these things happened for more reasons than I have ever been able to fathom. One thing I am getting a great sense of is how this is my own gathering of details. I am being given a gift to see things from all perspectives. There is something I am learning here, which I was unaware of previously. I am in this realm of God's space to help me understand how to truly forgive.

Yes, forgive! You see, I have overcome all of the injustices, or lessons if you will, and taught myself how to survive them all. What I had not known until this very moment was that I had never forgiven or forgotten the bad things in my life. I had always used the experiences to fuel myself toward surviving and conquering, knowing inside myself that I could do more than anyone had ever thought I could. I used the emotions of it all to change my own course in life. I did not want to be seen as a victim of my circumstances through other people's choices so instead turned them into something that only made me stronger physically, mentally, and emotionally, however I never truly forgave anyone for their wrongs against me until this moment.

I understand now. I will never forget the most important memories of my life experiences because they are mine to learn from. These defining life experiences give me the knowledge needed to help others. These memories also allow me to have my gut instinct which helps me avoid being victimized in these ways again.

Forgiveness. I never would have thought of forgiving any one of these people for the traumatic abuses they each inflicted upon me during my life. I have forgiven people for the small stuff such as a white lie, an inadvertent wrong, a bullying moment. But forgive something big like this? I am in awe at the reality and scope of what this true forgiveness means.

I used to think forgiving was forgetting and since I was unable to forget I could never forgive. Therefore, I shaped my life around the memories, not forgetting and never forgiving. I found a way to move on in quite profound ways, or so I thought.

How does God forgive us for our sins in life? The comparable of me forgiving these atrocities was unthinkable. I am not God, but I am a child of God created in His image, and therefore it is only right that He should show me how to truly heal from these experiences. I have no excuse. I have to forgive, but how?

Truly forgiving my transgressors means I will no longer hate them for what they have done to me. With that forgiveness true healing will come. I will be able to better help others when I show them how to redefine their victimizing experiences with true forgiveness and lead them on a greater path of healing.

I made my decision and forgave each of them individually for what they had done to me. After all, I was in a review of my life here in this majestic realm and I did not want to waste a single moment of what was being gifted to me.

Just as times before the soul light surrounding me becomes even brighter. The music changes to a higher octave and I can feel the excitement of the others who are present. It is as though I have just made the biggest decision of my life and yet, I am here standing in my death.

The moment I announce my true forgiveness I feel as though a million pounds are lifted from my soul. I know then that never forgiving was holding me back from my truest potential. It no longer matters to me whether they were sorry for what they had done to me. That is for them to account for someday. Today is for me, to truly hand my pain and suffering over to God, to ultimately and truly forgive, and I do.

26

Runaway

I have no idea the reasons but for a short time I was able to move in with my grandparents. I will say this was the calmest and most lovingly peaceful time in my life. I loved them so much and I was finally nurtured and loved without fear of any violence. I was able to join some extracurricular activities at school and felt normal for the first time in my life. I adored every moment gifted to me with them. I was thirteen and in a new school and I actually felt like the luckiest girl on earth. Until the day I turned fourteen and had to move back home.

By this time I had become hardened to other people's emotions and I only wanted to get on with my life. Moving back into another crazy home situation made me live in constant fear and anger again. It was a new kind of rage we lived with now. Our home life was in chaotic turmoil. We had a new stepdad who was scarier than anyone I had ever encountered. The fact that he was bigger, stronger, and a severe alcoholic made him even more frightening. I thought I knew anger from before but there was no one in comparison to this man. He would go into flat out insanely crazy rages and fists would fly at anyone who dared to stand in his vicinity. He could be an incredibly nice person one moment and in the next would throw dumbbells from the weight set at anyone close by. Each day was a mystery as to which side of him you would encounter. It was hard enough being in junior high and adding this kind of uncertainty to my life made me incredibly more stressed. It wasn't always bad between us but I quickly learned to stand up for myself again, as well as my siblings. He was not all accepting of my defiance or independence. Things went downhill for us fast and at age fourteen I became a runaway. I first tried to go back to my grandparents' house but was told they were not allowed to let me move back in with them. I presume everyone thought I would return home if they didn't let me stay with them. They were all wrong because I was so sick of that destructive way of life. I knew I would rather starve than ever go back. My mind was made up, so I disappeared into the city. I think most people around town assumed I had gone to my dad's in Alaska. It's hard to imagine how I thought having nothing was better than what I had been living with.

For quite some time I slept in a gazebo at the park in the center of the city, wandering around and eating what I could from wherever I could get it. I did get one job, which I promptly got fired from for lying about my age. I wanted to work and earn money but you had to be sixteen and I was two years too young. There were times when people would let me stay with them, would feed me and let me borrow clean clothes while I washed mine and showered. It was crazy how I didn't care if I had a roof over my head. I had peace and quiet in my life and mind. I was never really afraid because I already knew the worst things to fear in life. I was finally strong and old enough to have a choice and I chose not to live like that any longer.

I have always been so grateful for the people who tried to help me through those really tough times. Each of them has gained a special place in my heart, and I will carry their kindness with me forever. Most of them were aware of who and what I had run away from. Many of them knew firsthand about the intense anger of my stepfather and why I was running from him. The knowledge helped them have some extra compassion for my situation.

I was blessed for a short time to stay with a kind girl I had met through other friends. She had a small room the size of a walk-in closet which she turned into a room for me. It wasn't much, but I appreciated it more than anyone would ever know. It was starting to get really cold at night and she didn't want me sleeping in the park. During this time I found a note and bag of groceries which was left on the porch of the apartment. It was from my grandma and Papo. They had found me and knew I was alright but wanted to make sure I had enough food to eat.

There were three different people over a year's time who allowed me to move in with them and not have to live on the streets. I babysat, cleaned, and helped with chores to earn my keep. Despite their kindness, this was not the way I wanted my life to continue and God took the situation into His own hands.

It was November 8th, 1984 when a frantic knock rang through the apartment. The neighbor had found a note on the door addressed to me telling me to get to the hospital. My grandmother had suffered a heart attack. Papo had sent someone to bring me the news.

Standing here with her again in the realm of Heaven I felt the love she had and still has for me. I wish with a heavy heart that I had been able to stay with her at her house instead of how I had been living. I would have loved to share her last months with her. Had I been stronger I would have insisted on staying. Why? Why were they not allowed to let me live with them?

It had been decided that if I weren't allowed to go there then I would surely find my breaking point and go back home. Well, that never happened. Instead I found my surviving point and defied all odds to never return to the chaos that existed there.

From Heaven I watched the emotional breaking points of our family as they all said their goodbyes to her. I saw myself sit beside her bed, holding her hand and caressing her skin while the machines pump air and beep softly as they are keeping her alive. I saw myself lean close to her, kiss her cheek and whisper a heartfelt "I love you" and gave her my permission to go home to God and Jesus. I felt her hand jerk with a sudden movement then relax. I looked at my uncle, "Did you see that?" At that moment I knew she was gone, that her soul had left her body. I leaned forward and sang a soft hymn close to her ear, then the tears poured down my face.

At this point in my Life Review I turned to look at her heavenly essence. "Grandma, did I whisper the right thing? I have always wondered." The light surrounding her became even brighter, as did her smile, and she confirmed for me, yes, she loves me too and yes, it was right for me to give her a blessing for her journey to Heaven.

My beautiful grandmother was the one thread, the fundamental strength that held our entire family structure together. Each of our roads home always led back to her. She was the definition of Heaven's pure love and the truest form of kindness. It was heartbreaking still as I watched even though I was standing beside her. The amount of pain I experienced from the loss of her in my physical life left a gaping wound; a hole so large I didn't think it would ever heal.

I looked at her and she knew how much I loved every part of her soul. She was beautiful, and I am the lucky one for knowing her love and kindness in my life. I know now that she was an instrumental piece to the puzzle of my survival and she gave me strength and hope, even when I didn't know it was happening. I never told her everything that had happened to me but on that day in Heaven she had been present for the review of it all. I could see something like blessed wonder for my situation shining from her. My grandmother knew I had survived and had broken the cycle, and most importantly, she knew I had chosen to truly forgive.

27

Grief and Guilt

The first couple of weeks after my grandmother's funeral were a blur. Her loss could be felt at every moment. Her absence encompassed everyone. She was known and loved by so many. We all felt the void created by her absence. Papo was taking the loss of his true love the hardest. I could see the depth of his pain through his eyes and feel his loss. I couldn't stand him being alone and I knew he needed someone to help him hold it together. I made my decision and I moved in with him, without permission from anyone. I cooked for him, did his laundry, and I slept on the floor beside his bed for weeks. I held his hand at night as he sobbed uncontrollably from his painful loss. I hugged him and would tell him she could hear him; that she was still with us in spirit. I would silently cry with him as he would beg God to take him, too. I would tell him all the reasons he needed to stay. I would let him tell me all his favorite memories of her and rock him back and forth as his body was wracked with sobs. He couldn't see how he could ever survive without her by his side. She was so young, only fifty-two, and he had been unable to save her. Papo had survivor's guilt. He could not understand why God took her and not him. He thought she had had more to offer people in life than he did.

I was there to help and I wasn't going to let him die on my watch. He still had life left to live, whether he could see it or not. I needed him to live.

By the end of the holidays things got very quiet around there. Papo and I would go out and gather pick-up loads of firewood. We worked on cutting kindling bundles in the garage, as well as gathering and crushing cans for him to turn in for the aluminum. I was trying to get his routine back on track, to fill his days with activity and try not to think about his loss. Slowly, over a four month period, Papo was able to start healing.

I would notice him staring off at nothing while sitting at the dinner table. I'd ask if he was alright and he would smile. That's all, just smile. This went on for a couple weeks and one afternoon while cutting wood we took a coffee break. He had that smiling look on his face again. Papo paused, looked at me and said he wanted to thank me. I looked at him in wonder, "For what?" I asked. He answered, "You. You saved my life." As tears escaped his eyes I smiled, shook my head and said, "Papo, you saved mine first. I was only doing what I learned from you, paying you back for what you've done for me."

From that day on Papo and I had a bond that neither time nor distance could ever break. No matter where I would show up to surprise him he would hug me a good five minutes and thank me again, every single time, for saving his life as I would again thank him for saving mine. He shared this with anyone present, telling them I wouldn't let him die, even when he had wanted to.

28

An Unexpected Gift

My grandmother envelops me in her heavenly light once again, for she knows how hard I fought to keep Papo alive. She also knows how hard it was for him to lose her and how he needed strength like he'd never had before. I am grateful to have been chosen as the one to give him that strength, as I hadn't realized until now that Heaven had a hand in the situation.

I have more visitors as I stand here in my Review. I am so delighted to see each of them here, as it has been a very painful road to my own healing place. You see, shortly after my grandmother's unexpected heart attack and death, I tragically lost three very dear friends in the five months following. The first was killed in a vehicle rollover, the second in a plane crash, and the third to suicide. Three young men who had their whole lives ahead of them, gone; erased from my life in an instant.

Exuberant excitement fills me at this unexpected gift. They each had meant so much to me, in such different spectrums of my life. Two were the big brother protector types and one a kindred spirit from his own abusive past. I had a genuine connection to each of them individually during my life and am grateful for the time to reconnect in this realm.

I have to give the healing grace to God here for getting me through these tragedies and loss. You see, He gave me Papo to focus on. I found myself healing through my own grief as I was telling Papo every positive thing I could think of about Heaven. In the end, I was given the healing tools needed for both of us to carry on in life. For me, the loss of one person was bad enough but four tragic deaths could have been catastrophic for a young person with no direction. I prayed every day for the guidance I needed to save him from also dying. In the end, it healed us both.

29

Independence

I moved on with my own life the following spring once I was certain Papo would be okay without me. I knew it was time to get my life back on track. I went to Alaska, enrolled in school, got two jobs, and buckled down to get myself caught up. I moved into a hotel in town named The Lodge and even though it was just a room with a bed and bathroom it was my own space. I would go to school in the mornings, work at the cold storage de-sliming and cleaning fish in the afternoons and waitress at night, studying whenever I wasn't busy. By the following spring I got a job with a small airline and was able to quit cleaning fish, though to be honest I did enjoy the work.

I felt very blessed to have fishermen, loggers, even the telephone man help me study for my classes, and I was able to test out and graduate early. That summer I went on my first commercial halibut fishing trip. What an amazing experience.

My life was going better than it ever had and I was excited for my future. I was only sixteen at this time and although other people thought I had no idea about life, I felt I had already seen enough of it to fill three lifetimes. All I wanted was to not be associated with my past and to be given a chance at my own future.

I rented a place in Juneau and finally had a home of my own. I worked a 5:00 a.m. to 1:00 p.m. shift in Juneau, then would board a plan for the quick 20 minute flight to the island just off shore and work a 2:00 p.m. to 10:00 p.m. shift, close that airport, hop on the last flight back to town, go home and do it all over again the next day. I was able to save a significant amount of money and felt proud of how far I had come in a year and a half. After sleeping in the park and in other people's places for so long it felt good to be able to take care of myself.

There were still those who judged me for where I had come from but I no longer cared about what anyone else thought of me. Walk a day in my shoes then you can judge. For me, I just felt damn lucky to have survived my tragic life thus far.

By the fall of my seventeenth year I moved to Arizona with a boyfriend I had known for a while and spent the next several years dating off and on. We were in love and I cherished our time spent together. We had a lot in common and enjoyed doing many outdoor activities together. I married and divorced him in the same year, for reasons that aren't perfectly clear to me even today.

I will say this: I seemed to have had the same problem as so many of the other women in my family history. Call it codependency, compassion, or even a challenge, but I really thought I could be the fixer. I had experienced so much in my short life and didn't see this as something impossible. I had a tendency to think I could make other people see the beauty in life as I saw it and always believed I could help others become better people. It was as though I had been put into their life for a reason and I thought the reason was to fix them.

I guess I learned quickly enough the only person in this life that I had the ability to fix was myself. The only person who would ever look out for my best interests in life was me. I could never make somebody feel or see things the way I did. We each have our own view through life, as we each have our own path of experiences to walk. Once this realization sank into my mind I knew it was time to go.

Maybe those who judged me were right; maybe I was too immature and too young. It really doesn't matter now. I moved on in my life and became much more conscious of what I was looking for and what I would accept in my life from other people in the future.

By this time I was twenty-two years old and needed to get my life on track again. I'm not even sure where it all went wrong, or what was missing in my life, but something made me realize I no longer wanted to accept the way I was living and knew this was no longer where I needed to be. I left Arizona, went back north, visited my family and friends, and on a whim joined the United States Army. I wanted and needed a change. I still hadn't found what I was looking for in life and had to be willing to walk away from everything and everyone I knew in order to find the person I was destined to be.

I believed in the path of my "meant to be purpose" in life. Call me silly but I knew I had to be willing to "Let Go and Let God"; let Him steer the compass for a while in my life. It was just something I knew I had to do, which all brings us back to that day in Heaven. It will forever be known as my "Interception of Life."

30

Talking with Angels

Those who passed before me have now moved back into their places and I am left standing in front of the three Angels in white robes. My Life Book has turned the pages of my lifetime and have shown me all I needed to know at this time. I can see the words have ended on one page and observe the blank page next to it. I look up at them in silent wonder.

My first sincere question is, why? Why, did any of this have to happen? What am I missing? I feel like I am only getting part of my story and I don't have the final chapter to my life.

I am told it is true, there are portions of my lifetime left unseen. I will not see the reasons unless they are revealed to me during those other people's lifetimes.

"How am I to know that now when I am here with you in Heaven? Shouldn't I be able to know their reasons for what they did to me now?"

"Yes, you raise a genuine point with your inquiry, however they have not passed from their lifetime to give an answer to your question. They may still have time to tell you themselves in person."

"In person? I really don't comprehend any of this."

"What we can help you understand is this: your young life has meant a great deal to many people, both here and there. You have been watched over by many along your life journey and it has, at times, saddened even the strongest of us. We here have waited for this day to come. Today, we have intercepted your life and you will have choices of your own to consider very soon."

31

Standing with God

I feel everything around me change now; the brightness, the vibrations, the sound of the music, and the light, oh how it shines like the brightest star you have ever seen!

My Father, God in Heaven, I am home and I am being encapsulated in His most magnificent healing light. My arms spread wide as I take this energy into my soul.

I close my eyes at the brightness of Him and allow myself to feel the full love light of God encompass me. It is brighter than all the stars above, stronger than the heat of the sun, more peaceful than a morning rain, and more beautiful than all the flowers I have ever seen in bloom. It is more majestic than the sight of a murmuration of starlings in rhythm with each other, softer than the flight of the most delicate butterfly, grander than the majestic beauty of an eagle as it soars through the sky. He is everything. Every beauty He has ever created is assembled within Him and He fills me to overflowing with this amazing and powerful healing love.

I feel the worthlessness, doubt, and all of my negative abuses dissipate from my soul. It was so simply washed away, as if He healed me from the pain of it all with a single thought. As I stand before Him after my Life Viewing I ask, "Father when will I be judged?" His words are as clear to me now as they were to me then.

He says, "My child, I have felt your pain. I have witnessed the traumas, the tragedies, the events that have now come to define who you have really become. Why then, would I judge you? You have never lost your faith in who I am, as I have never lost faith in you. You have never turned your back on me or another living soul in need. You have not disappointed me. I will not judge the personal lessons put upon you. You have survived them to become who you are as you stand before me this day. I have always known who you were. I have always known who you could become. I have always known this day would arrive. I have always known you would stand before me with a choice that will only be yours to make this day. It should not be so surprising how I have chosen this day for you. I am well aware of the outcome of your life and today I present to you a choice. Your choice is to crossover to the eternal realm of Heaven, into my kingdom and be fully accepted into your afterlife here with me. Or…"

I am transfixed by my conversation with God. My attention is placed directly on His words to me, seeing nothing and feeling everything until that lingering question, and I feel everyone move in a little bit closer. It is as though I can sense all of the energy lights get a little bit brighter and the soft musical notes become a little sharper. I hadn't even noticed there was heavenly music playing in the background of our conversation. I feel my soul start to shine ever brighter and my energy makes me rise a little straighter. A tingling rush of excitement passes around all who were in attendance. They are waiting. I look at the Angels to my right where they are holding vigil over my Book of Life. As I glance over toward the Book I see it then, the blank page. The page next to it had ended where we left off in my life at the exact moment when I hit the ground and was lifted out of my body.

Why do I need to make a choice? Of course I am here, I am home. Who would ever want to leave? Do we all get a choice?

I am confused for a moment then asked no one in particular, "Why is my page blank?" The Book is so big it makes my blank page stand out so starkly next to the fully lived page facing it.

"I know you can help others. I have watched you heal through your own tragedies. I know you will be able to connect with those who have stopped believing, to inspire those who are struggling and walk beside and assist those who have lost their way. I know you can teach them about forgiveness and help them find their healing path. I ask this of you, for I know you can do this without judgment."

"Father, why me? I am nobody. I am not a minister, a leader, I am nothing extraordinary. Ordinary, really, although I feel quite spectacular here but back there in my real life I wouldn't know where to begin."

"My child, you will not be alone, nor have you ever been. I would not give this choice to you if I did not believe in you. This review has not been to set you up for failure but rather to give you knowledge, strength, and confidence to carry you through. I will tell you this, there will be challenges and pain; these things cannot be stopped. However you will, as you always have, turn this experience into another surviving accomplishment and others will be inspired to survive their pain through you. You have a beautiful soul, one which others are attracted to, and through your own healing process others too will allow themselves to heal. So many have lost hope and are in need of assistance to find their way into their faith again. There are lives to be saved and I know you can help me with this."

Let me say this, when God in Heaven told me He knows I can accomplish something in life, even to this magnitude, I am simply stunned. My soul bows before Him, and without another thought of doubt I knew I could do it. I knew I would go back and give His request of me, everything I had, even if I died trying, for I already knew where I would go when my journey was over.

"Yes," I say, "I will do it. I will return. If I can save only one person's life from their pain and heartache, share my experiences with them, show them survival can be acquired, then any pain I endure from my new tragedy will be worth it."

He spreads his light outward opening His arms and says, "My child, you will help and save many."

118

32

Interception of Life

At any point in our lives anyone one of us could experience an "Interception of Life". What I mean by this is something happens in a split second that is so life-altering it changes the very core existence of a person. It can variably be caused by many different things, for example the death of a loved one, a divorce, a traumatic experience, something done against you, or possibly, the death and return of your own true self. For me that is exactly how I viewed my life and death event. It was an interception of my life. The moment the lightning bolt hit me it changed me from who I was to who I came back to be. I returned with only partial memories of my previous life and yet I knew there was so much more to who I was before that day occurred. I couldn't put two plus two together to even get a glimpse of what was missing. It was just a vast empty space in my memory, yet I knew I was missing a great deal of the previous me.

My death, Life Review, and conversations with God and Angels, as well as my return to life became my only memories. What life experiences remained were left there for very specific reasons, so I would be able to relate to others and help them survive their most devastating interceptions in life. By saying this I am showing you why I was left with what I thought were only broken memories of myself. Each broken part was something I had survived to share with someone else in need. Those returned memories were my gift from the other side of life, from Heaven, that were left intact for one sole purpose: to help others heal as I had taught myself to do after each one of my traumatic experiences.

The view of my life as I was shown on the other side was an amazingly beautiful scene, even though it was interlaced with my own very personal life tragedies. The beauty of it came from my faith and perseverance to survive. It was quite magnificent to see my own life through an outside perspective. I was able to see why and how I became the faithful soul I am today. It was because I had one of two choices: grow up allowing myself to be the victim, or know I could be the survivor of my own life journey. I could learn my lessons from it all or I could let it tear my life apart. I could allow these tragedies to define me, or I could learn from them and redefine my life because of them. Obviously, I chose to be the survivor every time though never once was it easy to overcome the situation I faced. It took work and it took time but I never stopped trying to conquer my fears and overcome my pain. Not that I knew any of this as it was happening to me in real life. It became clear to me as I reviewed my life on the other side before God, the Angels, and my family and friends who had passed over before me. Standing there with them in the realm of Heaven, with pure love and knowledge swirling around me like the mist of the Northern Lights, I was shown the true God purpose of my life.

Since returning I have not deviated from the purposeful path on which God had reset my compass of life to follow. I acknowledge and honor His presence in my life, as well as His request, each day. There were extremely hard times while going through my physical, emotional, and mental healing processes but I did not give up. Inside I knew I had made a promise and I returned to my life with a purpose.

33

A Choice

In Heaven I had a feeling of weightless serenity which encompassed me. I was not alone, nor am I now. I felt safe and could sense the spirits of those I once knew who had crossed over to Heaven before me. One at a time our energies shifted. For me it was my physical heaviness that dissipated from my spirit then all at once I could see some of the others as they had been in their physical life form. It was as though an impression of their former self had been laid over their heavenly essence so I could recognize them now in their spirit form. I believe this happened to comfort me and to allow me to recognize them so I would not be afraid. Some of them were only partially physical looking as they were still encompassed by their heavenly light. It was an amazing sight to behold.

Being in Heaven was the most serene and glorious moment of my entire life existence. There I felt no pain; I felt only the splendor of love from everyone and my soul felt pure recognition that this was from where I had originated. I felt no doubt in what was happening to me. Glorious doesn't even describe it; it was truly the most magnificent place I had ever seen. With no question or doubt, I was ready to be in my afterlife where I knew I belonged. Finally, I thought, I was home.

Then the opportunity for a choice was given to me: step into my afterlife or choose to return. I had only one moment in time to decide this, which is the biggest decision of my entire existence.

I felt like a child with a Slinky in my hands as they showed me the weight and impact of my choice, back and forth, back and forth. My time, my life, your life, my help. My choice.

My choice, really?

In all honesty, I would have felt selfish had I chosen to stay in my afterlife for my own peace and tranquility. I would have felt less about myself than God already saw in me, even though he had given me a choice. I was given that choice because He believed in me, therefore how could I even consider saying no to Him? Even though being in Heaven was the most serene and magnificent moment of my entire life existence I could not have chosen any other outcome. I knew this was an important task and I could only give it everything I had.

34

My Return

I think I'm back. Or, am I?

I gulp a breath of air into my lungs and feel as though it just ignited a blazing inferno within my body. Suddenly, I feel the drops of water spatter my face from above and they make my body feel a spasmodic sensation. I have a heightened sensitivity to the physical contact of the drops and it shoots like electricity throughout my body. I can feel myself being moved very carefully and can sense multiple people around me. I hear other people's muttered voices talking in the distance, here and over there on the other side. I am flat and strapped to a backboard. It is a startling feeling to be confined inside my physical self again, as though I've been stuffed into a mayonnaise jar. I am unable to move freely and at will of thought as I was just moments ago, yet I am terrified at not being able to move. Am I paralyzed? Everything starts to spin as I feel a burning pain wash over me.

A misty fog of misunderstood confusion encompasses me. I am startled to hear someone calling my name demanding me to stay here, to not give up. I'm still not sure if I am fully back.

I did choose to come back though I feel I am still only half in each place. I can still feel them, the three Angels, surrounding me. They were each touching me as they laid me back into my physical body. That was my last clear view of them as I asked one if he thought I could do this. Maybe I'm not the one. He whispered back that they would be with me to help when I needed them to.

Maybe there was a mistake because I can feel someone hasn't yet let go of me. I can hear you but I can no longer see you. Is everything alright? Are we waiting for something?

All at once, like a hot light burning me with a dose of living reality, I realize I am indeed back. As the hands of Angels let go of me the pain was like nothing I had ever felt prior to or since that moment. Yes, I am here where it started. When, how long ago? I feel as though it could be close to forever since I have been gone but I am unsure how long it actually was. Time, where is it? Did time stop while I was gone? Did God just pause a break in my living life? Did He also freeze time for those below me as well? I'm unsure of everything although I feel as though I am existing nowhere and everywhere all at the same point in time. I no longer feel like I am who I was before. I can tell that some part of my existence has changed, like a veil hasn't quite closed. I can feel a connection to both sides, to life and afterlife. I must be in the right place but everyone is glowing far too brightly than how I know they should. Are my eyes burned? Is the sky brighter than normal? Are they crying, or it is raining?

Again I feel it hit my face. I am still confused. I want to sleep through this painful confusion and stop the pain from penetrating my heavenly glow.

"Hey Soldier- You can wake up now! We aren't going to lose you!"

God, please make him stop yelling. My head and face are burning. My body feels as though I have been ignited from the inside out. I feel broken or at least severely bruised from my landing. Landing from where, Heaven? Did I really just "land" from Heaven? Does it hurt this badly to land? Did they drop me or did I let go too soon? Wait, I feel the blackness again. This is all so confusing and painful, yet I want to laugh at the thought "I just landed from Heaven and oh, how I loved it there!"

"Beth! Come on back now! You have to stay with us. We are heading to the hospital. You need to breathe steady. We need to get your heart rate under control. Can you do that for me? Breathe, deep breath in. Everything is going to be alright. I'm not going to let you die on me today! Come on soldier, breathe! We are almost there. You are going to be okay. I'm here to help you. Come on soldier. Can you hear me? I'm not letting you die today. You can pick another day, but it's not going to be today."

Wait, what? Did he know about my choice? How could he have known? This isn't making any sense to me.

He is right; I am not going to die today. I suppose it means I really am back. Man, if only you knew I already did die today.

35

Panic

Yes, I came back. I agreed. I chose to return to my life today. If I could, I would smile at that memory but for now I can't. Nothing works in me yet.

Help me find my words. Where are my words? God this hurts so badly! Am I on fire here? What is burning on me? I can't move. Somebody please stop the burning sensation running around and through me, just make it stop. I'm panicking, I can't make it stop!

"Soldier, slow down! You have to calm down."

We've stopped moving for a moment and everything starts rushing in as panic envelops me. Oh no, now what? Please slow down. Stop moving so fast! I'm going to be sick. I cannot figure out the smells and the taste of burnt flesh and metal in my mouth. More so, I wonder for a split second how I even know that it's burnt and tastes like metal. Hey you, is my face burning? What burned? Am I glowing in a bright light?

I feel the light and even though my eyes are closed I still see brightness all around me. It must be the Angels here with me. Again, I feel the healing light wash not just over but through me. I feel the Angels here. Thank you for not leaving me! Can you hear me? Do you know what broke? I mean, I can feel that I am broken, but can't tell exactly what.

Where am I really? Not in Heaven, I know that from this unforgiving pain and this lost and heavy feeling. I am no longer as light as a bird or as free to float around as the Angels do. The Angels have returned me to my physical body. I hear one of them softly speak the words, "You agreed." Yes, I did, I agreed.

The brightness of their heavenly energy fades now, although I still feel their presence from a short distance away. I can hear muffled voices and the hospital personnel coming and going as fast paced activity is happening in every direction around me. I am trying to answer their questions but am stumbling upon my words. I am unsure if I am making any sense to them and immense fear takes over. I tell myself to pay attention but nothing makes complete sense. How much time has passed? Is it still today? It feels like I stepped out of my life for at least a lifetime. I still haven't opened my eyes.

Close to my face a woman's voice is saying, "Beth, you have been hit by lightning. We are trying to assess the damage and it will take us time to run some tests. We need to get your heart rhythm in check before we can make any decisions. You are a lucky girl, most don't make it. A very lucky girl, indeed."

I agree; I am a lucky girl. If only you knew. If only I could tell you how lucky I really am. I just got back from Heaven.

When I finally allow myself to open my eyes, it is not as bright as I thought it would be. Certainly not as bright as where I had just come from. The pain in my head is excruciating, unlike any headache I had ever felt before. Any motion or movement makes me want to vomit. I can't stand the feeling of anyone touching me. My skin is so hyper sensitive it's as though every nerve in my body is on high alert.

Hours pass and other soldiers from my unit come to the hospital to visit and check on me. I am skeptical as to who they are and how they really know me. Immediately I start pretending I know what's going on, however to be honest I have no idea. At that moment I know I have lost part of my mind and memory and cold fear grips me. I start trying to figure out how to avoid looking like a crazy person talking about Heaven and angels. I can't tell them, they will never understand. I don't remember enough of my old self to allow myself to talk too much. It is such a confusing whirlwind of time and space, Heaven to Earth, and life to death and back again. The whole thing makes me dizzy just thinking about it. Now I have to figure out where I fit back into my own life without people questioning me, afraid they won't believe me anyway.

They are talking about me as though I can't hear them, though it doesn't matter anyway for now I am lost in my own pain and confusion. Some of the other soldiers are cracking jokes and laughing, trying to cheer me up as my stomach is turning inside and out with colossal dread leaving me ready to wretch. I am quivering inside from the pain. I have no idea how long this escapade goes on but I want to escape the spotlight.

A doctor is talking to my fiancé and my superiors about my condition, telling them how lucky I am to be here. They think I am going to be alright. There really isn't anything else that they can do for me at this time, so they have decided to release me. The doctors are sending me home.

Home. I open my eyes. "Good," I think to myself, "now they won't be able to study my answers to things." Wait, where is home? Well, let's just say this, home is not where I should have been, no matter where it was. I should never have been released from the hospital that night. I am one hundred percent certain of that.

36

Release

Today I understand how mysterious the side effects of lightning can be, however I am certain had the doctors actually asked me more meaningful questions or kept me overnight they would have seen my incompetence at doing the simplest of tasks. They also would have picked up on the fact that I was unable to comprehend most of what was being said to me. I truly felt like a foreigner in my own life. My physical assessment was complete, no broken bones, just an erratic heartbeat which should work itself out. No matter, I couldn't open my mouth at all, or think, or speak clearly, or comprehend even the smallest thing said to me. Oh my goodness, I was broken in so many ways it would be hard for anyone to ever understand the depth of my trauma.

We were told to follow up at the troop medical clinic the next day. We did, and in short order the hospital was unable to locate any of my paperwork. It was not even 24 hours later and none of it could be found. The search for proof of me being hit by lightning became a five month journey of horrors. I lived each day with erratic heartbeats which nearly made me sick every moment of every day. Confusion and incontinence put my confidence level at a zero. There was so much weakness throughout my body it felt completely foreign to me, as though it belonged to someone else. I felt helplessly detached from everyone and everything I was before. Intense headaches made my skull feel like it was exploding and would block my vision in both eyes, from top left to bottom right, forcing me to squat down and crawl along the floor as I would try to feel my way. I did not feel like a soldier any longer, but instead like a child struggling to focus on one tiny task at a time, all the while hoping I wouldn't pass out and die when my heart would decide to run a marathon while I was only standing. Sounds of jet engines screamed in my ears as the room would start spinning around leaving me holding onto anything I could grab, always hoping I wouldn't hit the ground and hurt myself further. What the hospital failed to recognize was this: I had a traumatic brain injury and had lost several memories of who I was and where I belonged. My brain didn't know how to communicate with the rest of my body and kept sending the wrong signals for walking, talking, even when I needed to use the restroom. There was severe damage to my left ankle and both feet. My jaw was seized shut and my mouth was burnt inside, hence the burning smell and metallic taste I kept experiencing. The lightning had entered my feet, picked me up and threw me several feet forward, then grounded and exited out my mouth.

It is important for me to remind you while in Heaven I was told I would experience a great deal of pain from this event in my life. Even with this knowledge I did agree to return. Never could I have imagined the enormity of the situation and how much it would affect my health and well-being. From where I had been standing in Heaven I felt nothing in the form of pain nor confusion or doubt about my ability to fulfill this request. The glorious freedom of being home and basking in so much love and heavenly light meant that my mind never quite captured the true depth of its meaning.

In my darkest despair I never once thought of taking my own life, nor did it cross my mind to wish I had chosen not to return. Losing a dear friend to suicide in my teens was the lesson I needed during my Life Review to remind me during my most pained moments. What did make me reevaluate my choice of returning was my extended incapability of actually accomplishing the grand task which I had agreed to do. My return introduced me to the true meaning of suffering, which was utterly confusing until I realized I was allowing myself to only see my situation as a hindrance. I was equating my emotional, mental, and physical pain to suffering and also focusing on my inadequacies at moving forward in my task, when I should have been re-defining it as my true life path to walk. I already knew how to do these things, what I needed to find was a new direction. I had to find a path for healing my wounds the best I could and survive this just as I had in the past.

The day I decided to look at my life and allow myself to truly see the way I viewed my unfortunate situation I knew I had to make a change. I had only been viewing it as a negative but made a conscious choice to lay it out on paper so I could view it from every perspective. I literally made myself step out of the emotion of my own connection to it. By taking this different approach, I was able to reevaluate the way I viewed and related to my situation. I could analyze it from an outside point of view as if it weren't my life but someone else's entirely. A strategy I would strongly advise if I were helping another person through this awful tragedy is to study it and come up with solutions. Through this method I found my new healing path. My injuries no longer had control over me; I had taken control of them and from that day forth my suffering improved.

These changes didn't happen overnight. First I had to alter the way I thought every moment of every day. Habits are very hard to break and for my traumatized brain they were sometimes even harder to retrain. I had become accustomed to only seeing what was not working right for me, instead of reminding myself what was still intact. It was a challenge for sure. I knew bits and pieces of my previous self but mostly it was an instinctual knowing of who I would have been before. Instead of trying to find my way back to the old me again, I decided to take a new approach and become who I thought I would have wanted to be. With my memories of Heaven and a brain that would forget things in mid-sentence I set forth and gave myself permission move on and do the best I could with what tools I had gathered. I stopped making excuses for my lack of knowledge and faced the fact that it was gone. I couldn't go to the local market and buy any of it back. I was not going to allow myself to make more excuses as to why I couldn't do what I came back here to do.

One day I asked myself, "If I died today, would my return experience on Earth have been worth it?" I did not like my own answer to that question. I knew I could do better and knew more than anyone how Father Time knocks on everyone's door at some point in their lifetime. After all, it is the cycle of life. In one moment, boom! Punch your number, your time is up and your life is over. Welcome to your Life Review. What did you do to make a difference while you were there?

No way, I had been there, done that, and certainly wasn't going to waste another minute of my life finding reasons not to get something done. I had wasted enough time. It was time to fulfill my destiny.

I had already learned firsthand how the status of wealth you achieve on Earth does not give you a higher step up the ladder into the threshold of Heaven. It is what you did on Earth to help others, without expectation or judgment, which grants your soul permission to enter a higher realm of enlightenment once you arrive back home to Heaven.

37

Doubting Myself

There were many times over the years when I questioned my ability and strength to accomplish my heavenly task. Each day I found myself praying so much it became more like daily conversations with God and the Angels who had helped me. At times I was so desperate to understand how I would ever survive the painful outcome to my physical body. My inability to control the pain was holding me back in such profound ways. I was definitely becoming more isolated and didn't want to participate in any regular life activities. I avoided being around people who knew me before my accident and found myself unable to let people into my life for any extended period of time because I didn't want them to see how much of me was missing and how truly broken I was.

On July 19, 1993, almost exactly one year to the day after first being struck by lightning, I had an appointment with a psychologist. We had been working on ways to help me move on from my experience. In the year since being struck I had such a hard time with the loss of my own ability to complete the smallest of tasks. Doctors at Walter Reed Army Medical Center had treated me and I had since enrolled in school back at Ft. Benning to help me relearn what I had lost. Unfortunately, I was making slow progress and was advised by my doctor, in an encouraging way, to "be a soldier, suck it up and get past it". It had been a year and it was time for me to face my fears. I was advised to go home, watch the incoming storm and get my courage back.

From the damaged state of mind in which I existed I thought nothing about questioning his advice and did as I was instructed. I went home, took off my boots, rolled up the pant legs of my BDU's, opened the French doors at the front of my house and stood on the threshold. Trying to be the brave soldier I was before I watched as the storms rolled in.

Neither the psychologist nor I could have known his advice could have killed me that day, or how it would change the healing course of my life for years to come. As I watched the storms I could hear the thunder and started seeing flashes of lightning. I told myself over and over again, "Be brave, be a soldier, you can do this" because I wanted to feel like myself again. At the time I was not particularly frightened because I knew I had survived being struck before and really wanted to get better. Within minutes the sheer power of the storm was overhead and I could feel my feet and legs becoming wet from the windblown rain. In unison I heard the thunder and felt the hot bolt of lightning hit. At the same time I was once again lifted off the ground, only this time I was thrown backward about nine feet into my house. I had been hit again. I did not lose consciousness this time but I did feel the shock of electricity go through my body and felt extreme fear tear through my mind as I let out a scream which I can still hear in my memory today.

What are the odds of this scenario happening? There was no possible way for any of us to have known it would turn out like that. Unfortunately, I became extremely angry, but also became terrified of it ever happening again. Even though I knew it wasn't the doctor's fault I felt it wasn't my fault either. I could not fathom how I was to make myself move forward from this point. That is when I lost the last remaining strength and confidence I had left. I was completely crushed; mind, body, and spirit. Time became a blank space and I have no idea how many days, weeks, or months passed with no memories. To this day I have flashes which are vague and shadowed, as if a protective shield was erected to keep me from being traumatized further. I don't think my mind could take any more and it just shut down.

We had no idea how much physical damage this strike had added to my already ailing body because I was still going through so much evaluation and rehabilitation from the first one. However, I can tell you the second strike nearly destroyed me emotionally. My anxiety was not so bad from the first strike but the second solidified a deep-seated fear in me which took years to get control over. I doubted my own sanity for not challenging the doctor's advice that day, as well as my ability to make a rational decision that would not inadvertently do me more harm. I questioned my heavenly experience as to whether I really could accomplish what I had agreed to do. I worried whether

God Himself was angry at my progress and mostly wondered how would I ever overcome the fear of lightning striking me again and be able to do what He asked of me. Every day I prayed for peace in my own mind and for strength to overcome my fear. I held onto the memory of Heaven and my Life Review and knew somehow and someway I would find my way back to my life here on earth.

Yes, I know I've been hit by lightning twice and you would think that surviving would be enough to describe my life story. The truth is what really defines me is how I crawled through the abyss of pain and fought my way back from the darkest recesses imaginable, all because I believe in a promise I made to someone I cannot see nor prove even exists. However, I know to the very core of my soul the reasons He asked me to return and I will not let Him down.

Before I knew it, three years had passed and I felt like I had done nothing toward my promise to God. I was at my lowest breaking point in my entire life and still couldn't get a firm grasp on a single moment of it and figure out a way to move forward. From my visit to Heaven I knew I possessed the ability but I could not find a single puzzle piece to start the outline of this new picture. Nothing made sense to me any longer and I really started to question my own strength. It was at this time when I finally started getting medical attention for the injuries I had sustained from the lightning. My life in and out of the hospital and physically trying to relearn things took precedence over my emotional recovery. First was the reconstruction done to the tendons and ligaments of my left foot and ankle. Approximately four and a half inches were taken from the outside area and reattached to strengthen my left foot in order to give me some stability to walk correctly again. There was severe nerve damage and vessel flow problems and I was soon diagnosed with Raynaud's disease, a disorder of the blood vessels in hands and feet, and had the first of my toes amputated. Over the course of the next twenty years I would have all ten toes removed through five different surgeries. There was also significant damage to my jaw from the lightning exiting out my mouth and I have had more than a dozen surgeries to help me be able to open my mouth wider than my pinky finger. For a very long time I could not chew large bites of food nor could I fit anything in without trying to pry it open. At the time of my injury I had weighed 158 pounds and over the first two years was down to 103 pounds. The fact that my thyroid had become overactive and my inability to eat large amounts of food was working against each other and I could not gain weight.

During this time my heart rates had still not found a normal rhythm. I dealt with extremely erratic rhythms that left me feeling like I was going to die from a heart attack on a daily basis. It was all so confusing and unsettling, for I could do nothing to make them function at a normal rate. Then again, nothing in my life was anywhere near my normal any longer. I still deal with this dysfunction but I do not let it panic me any longer. This irregularity has become my new normal.

Finally came more counseling, which honestly should have been the number one priority since I was not prepared for the emotional roller coaster of my return. I was unsure of how to share this information with my friends and family, let alone with doctors. On one hand I needed them to know and understand, on the other I was petrified to share any of it with them. Bottom line, I didn't want anyone to think I was insane.

It didn't take the doctors long to diagnose me with severe depression, anxiety, and post-traumatic stress disorder. I was so angry at the labeling of my situation that I almost didn't go back. After all, I had died from a lightning strike and came back to help people and now I was being told I had all of these disorders. To label a person in what I perceived to be such a negative way made me want to cry, and for hours I did, thinking I would never stop. How had I let myself get to this place? Sitting in my wheelchair looking out the front window of the house I knew I was wounded in more ways than one. I couldn't see the daylight that was shining through the window. Enduring the torment of my own pit of hell I didn't know where to start to find myself again. Thinking of Noah being stranded on the Ark I wondered how he kept his faith. Even though for me it was far longer than forty days I couldn't allow myself to lose mine, knowing that faith and understanding of what happened to me was all I really had left.

When the only real tie you have to your own life existence is your faith, that's when you know you are in something vast and deep. I couldn't touch or see it but I felt it and knew it better than anything else. Why everything happened the way it did I still don't understand but I never let it break my faith in my connection to God. I held tightly onto my faithful knowledge of what happened to me, knowing it was my only remaining lifeline.

Had I ever wanted to give up it most definitely would have been that day. A day worse than that in my entire life on

Earth I cannot recall, and I've had plenty of terrible days. I felt like I had indeed failed my purpose in life because not one thing I had ever survived remotely compared to my feeling of inadequacy that day. Depression, anxiety, PTSD; it all became too much for me to fathom. It was too many labels at one time and I was in too many broken pieces to see how to glue myself back together, even temporarily. My mind and body were shattered into a million pieces of broken glass.

Rarely do I allow myself to revisit these memories. When I do, I see myself sitting in that wheelchair, staring out the big window of my house and can see how fragile I really was and know that one wrong move could have scattered those broken pieces of me into a maze of shattered glass on the floor. I would pretend I was okay, would lie to myself and to others. I had a misguided sense of being a failure and had no way of knowing how to heal. I used to crutch around the house, so precariously trying not to fall though so many times I did. I would resort to scooting around on my bottom pushing a basket of laundry and, not being able to carry it down the stairs to the laundry room, would launch it like a bowling ball from the top, sit and scoot down the stairs, refill the basket and throw it again, often crying through the entire process. You could say I was really angry. I say I was frustrated, confused, and really, really scared; so extremely afraid that I would never find myself again. Sometimes I think it would have been better if I couldn't feel or remember that parts of me were missing. Even more, I couldn't do what I was meant to do and certainly didn't feel like the miracle other people said I was.

Many times when I allowed myself to feel inadequate for this heavenly return, or doubt my ability to accomplish things that seemed impossible, something supremely amazing would encompass me and remind me to believe otherwise. A voice would whisper from afar reassuring me of who I was and why I was here, reminding me not to lose my faith. I would persevere through all my brokenness and believe in something I could not see but remembered from a place far away. I would conjure the images of Heaven and remind myself of the peace and painless serenity I felt there in order to could get through the pain I returned to. Someday I would be back there again, I just needed to get through these obstacles, complete my task, and be ready when my time comes again.

I had heard people talk about being at rock bottom and I knew I was lower than that. I was referred to a new psychologist, but didn't want to return for more counseling because I couldn't handle the weight of one more grain of sand on my shoulders, the pressure of another diagnosis. I spent a week thinking of every excuse I could conjure in my head for a reason not to go. The entire week was spent scared and crying and nearly ready to explode at anyone who looked at me. Then, on the day of my appointment, I went. Thank God in Heaven I did. For hours I talked about what all had happened to me, how I got to where I was on this day, poured out all my fears and desperate feelings of failure to her, and explained the nightmares that persisted in my sleep and my total sense of failure. She listened, handed me tissues, and never once stopped or interrupted me. The flood gates inside me opened and carried all of my burdens back to God. That day I removed them and never allowed them back into my life. It was as though she gave me a life preserver and a hand to hold as she allowed me to release this awful sickness that was consuming my life. I learned that day what it meant to cleanse yourself of your emotions because I flooded the room in them. I didn't feel the tears would ever stop though when they finally did I was physically and emotionally drained. I didn't feel embarrassed or judged, only relieved for the opportunity to get rid of the pain and emotional turmoil before it killed me.

I had just been given the greatest opportunity, permission in a sense, to unhook the imaginary cart I hauled around with me. It had become too heavy for me to carry as it was overflowing with every painful emotion I hadn't yet dealt with. No longer did I need to carry the burdens contained in it, I had the memories and they would be enough to carry me through into this survival realm.

Over the next seven years I saw this counselor and she taught me to take everything one baby step at a time. That was all I needed to hear because I set my course of healing based on those words. Learning to read, write, walk, talk, potty train, and live again, one baby step at a time. When the pressure of being fixed all at once is removed from your shoulders, it gives you permission to focus on one tiny thing and work your way into the big ones. Small tasks to get me out of the house, such as grocery shopping, bill paying, and socializing without fear of getting struck by lightning again, were all taught to me. There were safe places set up around town for me to go to if it started storming. Basically, the counsellors and psychologists set up a safety net of sorts and allowed me no excuses not to go out of my secure environment. It was amazing to find some independence and start to build a new normal for myself. I was finally starting to feel like I could fulfill the promise I had made in my afterlife.

My realization of how I was trying to get back to the person I was before was one of my most enlightening moments since my accident. I hadn't recognized how I was trying to find my way back to who I was on that specific day before the lightning changed everything. In hindsight, that is precisely where most of my emotional dysfunction went wrong. I didn't know I couldn't be who I was before but that is exactly where I kept trying to go. Not one of us, not even a perfectly healthy, undamaged person can ever be who they were yesterday. It took six years for me to see the reality of this in conjunction to my situation. When I truly saw it, it was like a curtain was lifted and I could see my future in life again. I knew that I could only be who I really was today and tomorrow I would be different. Even the years I spent stranded I was a different person each day because I could see how I got worse instead of better. Instead I focused on those baby steps and chose one thing at a time to get back to an acceptable normal for the new me. Sometimes I could fix or change something in a day, other times it could take a year or more to make progress, but I never lost sight of what I knew could be done. I gave myself permission to take the time I needed to get it right and did not give failure the option over surviving and succeeding.

I started to share my story as I went through my healing journey and opened up about my experiences never holding myself back. I was not going to allow others to have any power over me and my progress. Fear and judgment were my biggest obstacles but I pushed them aside and allowed God in Heaven to lead me here on Earth. I knew with conviction my life had a greater purpose and that doubt and fear cannot be present when you truly have faith in God. That's not to say I don't still get judged, I do and it sometimes hurts deeply, however I often remind myself of how I felt His light fill me. That is all I have to think of when I am pained by someone's careless words now. Although, having felt pain like that reminds me to tread lightly when dealing with other people's feelings, as I would never want to leave another person feeling hurt in such a negative way. I suppose it once again solidifies the fact that we experience things a certain way to teach us some of our biggest lessons.

38

Special Visitors

During the weakest point of my journey I found myself in a really depressed state of mind. I would cry and question my ability to ever survive this darkness, let alone help others. I remember feeling so worthless and inadequate. Compared to the strong person I knew I once was now I was nothing. At night I would fall asleep with tears still wet on my face. You could say I felt defeated and I am pretty sure God and the Angels knew I had hit as low as I could possibly go.

Somewhere in my realm of sleep and emotional exhaustion, I felt myself walking down a path. I could see butterflies flitting around me and hear birds singing. There were people mingling with one another off to the sides. The colors were spectacular and I felt as though I had been here before but nowhere in my life could I remember seeing this place. There was a bench ahead of me and I gave into the urge to sit and relax for a while. I tilted my head back and allowed the warmth of the sunlight to wash over me as I breathed it in. It felt so good. It had been so long since I have felt warm inside and out. My body has been too cold for so long. I almost feel alive again as my skin tingles from the warmth. I had forgotten how it feels to be me. Where has the sun been? It's as though I haven't felt it in years. This is so great! I am loving the strength I feel again and wherever this place is I do not want to leave.

A moment later, I sense a shadow block the light from above and can feel someone looking at me. I force myself to open my eyes and a big smile engulfs my face. "Hello, again. How is this happening? Did I die again?"

He chuckles, and tells me, "No. We are just going to have a meeting to help you and remind you of your choices."

"Oh," I say and look around to see the other two coming toward us. "I know I haven't been doing a very good job of it. I am sorry. I'm not sure I can fix this and do what He asked me to do. I am probably disappointing Him."

"Not at all, you have had more to overcome through this experience than all your previous ones combined. We all knew it would be difficult as it was a grand task for you to take on. We were all aware of the challenges you would face after your return, however you must remember these too are lessons for you to gain knowledge and experience from. What you learn to survive you will share with others who need help too."

"Yes, I remember. I really thought it would be easy for me to get past it quickly and move into my helping phase. I just can't seem to gather myself together enough to get well. How

am I to help other people when my body and mind feel so broken? I really feel I am at a point of ultimate failure."

"We want you to remember something else. You agreed and chose to return in order to help others. You saw and felt the importance of this request. The Father, God in Heaven, chose you because He knew you were strong enough to survive this, just as you were shown in your Review all the ways you taught yourself to survive everything that was put upon you in your lifetime before this day. You did not live as the victim of your life. You saw nothing put before you as an obstacle but found an avenue to become stronger because of it. Your faith in Him has never wavered and neither has His in you. Do not start doubting Him now. There is no time for that, now is the time for you to show others how to survive."

"How? How do I help anyone, when I cannot figure out a way to help myself?"

"You stop doing it backward. You stop trying to put your old self back together. First, you help others and it will in turn help you."

"Are you serious? Has it really been that simple, so small of a detail? How could I have missed the idea of that?" Of course I knew why I didn't do it that way because I didn't want people to see the broken and vulnerable side of me. Everything in physical life is simple, really. It is just that human nature has a tendency to choose to make it complicated so the challenge becomes harder to overcome.

"Will you consider trying to heal through your pain this way, by finding a path from a different direction? Start helping

others on your journey. We do not want you to suffer, as it not necessary or beneficial for you any longer."

"So, that's it? I just decide and it will be done? I can start helping and sharing the message and my pain will be gone?"

"Yes and no. You start by doing what you came back here to do and your life will change. Your strength will grow stronger; however your pain will be with you until you return home. There is no way to erase these feelings since the damage to your physical body has already been done. Are you ready to move forward now into the next phase of your journey?"

"Yes, I suppose I am. Thank you for your insight and wisdom. I have missed and yearned for the feeling of Heaven ever since the moment of my return. This feeling I have now sitting here with all of you has given me a new sense of myself and has rejuvenated my spirit. It has reignited my soul purpose reminding me of the importance of my return. I needed this moment of clarity to balance myself again."

"Please remember you are never alone. We were chosen to assist you again through your darkest day. You may sit and bask in this light and when you awake, you will remember."

39

Renewed Purpose

When I awoke from my sleep the next morning, I did remember. Call it a dream, or a visit from the Angels on the other side, whatever suits you. All I knew for certain was a dormant part of me had been reawakened and I was ready to get on with the next chapter in my life.

The reality of knowing I had finally gathered the broken pieces of myself and had successfully put them back together as best as I could fit them opened a new door for me. I am no longer who I was before, nor do I try to be that person. I now know I am meant to be so much more.

Since the morning I awoke from this experience I have not deviated from the path I came back to walk. Around the world I share my story with any and all who want to hear or simply need it. No longer do I question the doors which open to new directions in my life for I simply know wherever I am meant to be God will lead me there. I do the best I can with what I have to work with and have definitely learned to have a sense of humor at the missing pieces in my life.

I have connected many dots in this new picture of my life and will be forever grateful for the struggles I went through, simply because they made me so much stronger than I ever was before. "Never give up" has become a mantra in my mind which serves me well as I endeavor upon things which I never would have thought possible in my situation and circumstance. By never giving up I have been able to show others that anything is possible.

There are so many answers to the question of why this happened to me and I have covered most of them throughout this story, but the number one answer is forgiveness. I had to learn to not only survive the tragedies of my life but to truly forgive those who hurt me in such damaging ways. I do not have to forget. As you can see, God left me with the memories which would most serve me on my journey toward helping others. He chose the highlights of my Life Review to teach me what I had survived, as well as what I needed to forgive. Forgiveness has lifted the burden off of my shoulders and allowed me to move forward in such profound ways. I do not worry what punishment will come to those who hurt me; I have forgiven and it is now in God's hands. What He chooses to do with it doesn't concern me any more.

I attained true poetic justice by giving true forgiveness to those who have harmed me in my life. By granting this forgiveness it releases any hold those wrongs may have had over me, for those who had a part in harming me still have to carry their burdens, as well as answer for their actions one day in their own Life Review. As for me, I am at peace and I have my freedom.

40

Destiny

There are those who choose to doubt my experience, as well as ones who like to judge it. Although it hurts me sometimes, it truly does not matter to me who believes for I already know God chose to trust in me. He believed in me enough to ask me to come back to help others without any personal judgment on my part. For having had this awakening I am a much healthier soul and will carry out what was asked of me until my last breath is taken and my soul once again is lifted from my physical body and returned to Heaven. When I stand before Him the next time I will know without a doubt that I did everything I was destined to do. I gave back to those in need and helped save the lives of others in their darkest moments, helped restore faith back into those who had lost it somewhere along the way. I will not fear that I lived an insignificant life but will know in the depths of my soul that I fulfilled my promise to

God and completed all of the tasks He put before me to the best of my ability. For those He chose to have an opportunity to have my help, whether I was able to walk beside them for an extended period of time or the ones I was only blessed to cross paths with briefly, I am thankful. In my soul I know I have served Him well.

These are the connections to Him which have kept me going throughout my own painful life lessons. I worry not for the physical ailments that plague my body for this shell is only the outer part of me. It is my soul which shines in the brightest light and sneaks its way through my scars so you too can catch a glimpse of this light He filled me with. On the days when the pain seems too much to handle I close my eyes and reflect on the beautiful love light He poured into me. I gather my faith and knowledge then pray for His healing light to wash over my pains again. For me, it works. For you, remember this: He filled this light inside you as well and you only have to remind yourself it is already there.

Epilogue

It is November 20, 2014. It has been twenty-two years and four months today since I was struck by lightning and my whole life existence changed. As I am preparing to release this, my second book, I recall what an extraordinary journey my life has actually been. It is still hard for me to fathom how I made it to where I am today, having to relearn my words and thought processes again. It gives me great confidence in knowing I can do just about anything I set my mind to these days, within reason of course. I know I can't make my toes grow back, or put my memories back in place, but can honestly say I wouldn't change a thing, for without every experience you have read about me I wouldn't be who I am today. I survived and conquered. I did the best I could do with what was left of me to work with. As I stand here today reflecting on my life journey I know one thing for certain: I am not a victim. I am one hundred percent a true survivor. Faithfully I have found my destiny path and am grateful to all who lifted me up along the way. The lessons I experienced all had a purpose. I have gathered the knowledge I needed to help people through their most traumatic and life suffering experiences. As I said to God that day in Heaven, "If I go back to help and save one person's life, my pain would be worth it", and He replied with his light spread wide, "My child, you will help save many."

And so my story goes. Each day I have found the way to do my best to help any and all who are searching for a kind word of encouragement or a hand to hold along their path to healing. It truly becomes a testimony of helping and saving lives. I am dedicated to fulfilling those words from God when He said that I would help save many.

There are so many differences between the girl I thought I wanted to be in life and the woman God knew I was meant to become. Occasionally, the fog clears and I get a glimpse of the girl I previously was but before I can elaborate the memories of her they disappear again into the abyss of my damaged brain. Although I can see some parallels to what memories I do have, I can also still feel the empty space. It sometimes still saddens me today to have people who knew me before talk about moments we shared while I still have no clue what they are talking about. I suppose that is why I moved so far away from where I lived before. I didn't know how to help people understand how much of me was missing when I didn't understand it myself.

As I allow myself this time to reflect on my accomplishments, I see that I have surpassed my own expectations. Twenty-two years and four months and I am still looking forward to what tomorrow will bring. My husband and I have been married for twenty-one years now. My children have found their own purpose and passion in life. I have given my time freely to so many and have shared my faith with any and all who have needed me. I expect nothing from others and only have a desire to help them find their healing path. Never did I imagine how it would feel when a person thanked me for saving their life but that too has happened many times over. I am left humbled in the knowledge that God was so right. If I had to say today what the best part of my life was, it would be dying and coming back to my pain because without it I wouldn't be able to connect in an understanding way and know how to help save another person's life.

These days, I am often asked what is most different about me. I can only describe it as everything. My thoughts, my actions, and even the way I perceive things are all different. No longer do I let the fuel from hatred cloud my mind; it is not what steers me toward the light. I have attained a higher understanding of forgiveness and without it I would not be where I am today. Letting go of my anger at those who hurt me in the worst way was as freeing as if someone gave me wings to fly. Grasping the full understanding of my journey of pain and using it to help others was an instant relief to my soul. I was given a gift from an outside perspective, a view of my lifetime and although I have no proof I can assure you I wouldn't be where I am today had I not experienced it. Through all my broken moments I have found I really do have a purpose for living. I am still a human being and I do still make normal mistakes. In no way am I perfect according to society's standards, nor do I strive to be. What I do strive for is to be the most honest and faithful person I can be. Even when I stumble or forget what I said yesterday, I live for today instead of being mad at my situation and struggles in life. I will never have all the missing pieces of me but I can build new things to replace the missing ones. Often I describe this as painting a new picture of myself. It allows me to accept myself for who I am today instead of yearning for the person I can barely remember.

Through my process of healing I see how each one of us has a pretty good understanding of where our level of faith lies within. Each one of us should feel an obligation to do everything in our power to help those who are struggling or just do not know how to find their faith again. It is up to each of us to lead others by example.

My journey back was to inspire others and to teach them to not allow themselves to live in the desolate isolation of their experiences but rather to redefine them into their moment of survival and triumph and help them rejoice in their knowledge and truly understand that God does not give you more than you can survive. He does not abandon you in your darkest hours but tries to release these burdens from you. Give them to Him. Park your overflowing cart of burdens and baggage on the side of the road. Leave the heartache of worries behind you. Give yourself permission to move forward in life and start living again. Be grateful, be inspiring and most of all, be someone whom others will aspire to be. The example you live by, without judgment, will be a life blessed by God.

Clarifications

I do not want to leave you with questions as to some of the people I reference in this book, as there are no names mentioned. I chose to not elaborate on my mother's birth father since he had no part in my Life Review. He has, however had an incredible impact on my life. When I was twelve years old we met and my life was connected to him from that moment forward. He had remarried, had children, and was very happy in his life. Also, having another grandmother in my life was like a gift from Heaven to me, since I lost mine at such a young age. This grandfather, my mother's birth father, was a rock for me to lean on and encouraged me to be everything I wanted to be in life. He was a veteran himself and he became the most instrumental person involved with getting medical attention for my severe injuries. He fully recognized my incapability to function as the person I was before. For the rest of my life I will always be grateful to him and know we will sit together again one day on the other side of life.

I would also like to add more clarity of my life with my mother. She was such a gentle soul, with a heart so big and a smile for everyone she ever met. A person could not help themselves from being drawn to her in ways that were indescribable. She had an energy most people were attracted to. You just wanted to be around her and share with her your most heartfelt pain, as though she had the secret answer to fixing what was broken. She had the ability to make a room light up and leave every person feeling as though they were brand new. Everyone that is except herself; she always had the hardest time believing in her own potential.

It is important to share this with you because in no way do I want this book to reflect a negative opinion on the memory of my mother. She was as much a victim in her life as I was in mine. She truly was an amazing person and I certainly inherited my kindness toward others from her. She had the biggest heart and freely gave to others without ever expecting anything return. My mother loved us with all her heart, right up until her last breath, and I am so grateful to have been present for every moment of her final four months of life, as well as when she departed on her final journey home. There was probably only a year's worth of days in my forty-six years of life where we didn't at least speak to each other on the phone. I truly wish I hadn't have let a day go by, however there were times it couldn't be helped. For instance, in basic training the drill sergeants didn't let you call home to your mom at the end of each day, no matter how badly you may have wanted to.

It is only my opinion, but my mother seemed to forever be looking for something no one else was ever able to see. I think she had a dream and could never find the avenue to bring it to fruition. If I had to describe her I would say that she shined like a star and wished she had the wings of a butterfly. She wanted so much out of her life, though many times she found herself at the bottom of the ladder. She always had at least one job and often found herself working more than one just to survive. Lazy was not a word in her vocabulary.

Mom was an extremely generous person and had been known to give her coat to someone who was cold and would herself go the entire winter without. She would give away her last dollar to anyone who needed it more than her and the door to our house was always open to friends and family alike. If you were hungry my mother would feed you. There wasn't anything she wouldn't pay forward to another human being. In truth, she was a pretty spectacular person for these kind gifts she shared, although I think her kindness sometimes made her a target. Most often, though not always, she would attract the most abusive kind of men in her life. When she did find a person who was loving and kind to her, she would find a reason to walk away. On one hand, I think she felt she didn't deserve such divine happiness, and on the other I think she was afraid of it.

Despite all of this, I truly believe the abuse my mother experienced as a young girl, not unlike mine, was her lifelong undoing. For some unknown reason she allowed herself to be broken down and abused time after time. She would find the most broken person and set forth trying to give them a better life. It was as if she needed to prove to herself, or to them, that they could be saved.

As I reflect back now, I can see she didn't know how to overcome her own life trauma, nor was she able to find the tools needed to heal her own pain. It was a revolving carrousel, a repeat of the same lesson over and over throughout her life. What was emotionally broken in her stayed broken for most of her years, though not all of them.

If you read my first book you know a little about how much we loved our Mom and what we did with her before she crossed over. She was diagnosed with metastatic cancer, her lungs were one hundred percent covered and she had tumors throughout her body, including seven in her brain. She was only fifty-seven years old.

We were able to spend four and a half glorious months making memories and healing our wounds together. The time God gave us with her was our ultimate blessing. My favorite moments were when she would ask me at bed time if I would share my story of Heaven and dying. We would talk about the crossing over, the Angels, my Life Review, the people on the other side who were present, and my time before God. I was able to help my mother find her peace before her passing. She had no fear and was looking forward to being in a place with no pain. Had I not died on that day long ago I don't think I would have had the words which were needed to prepare and comfort her; I would have only been able to guess. Even though I was not able to save my mother's life here on Earth, I do believe I was able to help heal a part of her soul before she departed. In the grand plan of it all we were able to give her the love she needed from each of us and know she really was blessed in her life.

We all miss her very much but it gives me great pleasure in knowing where she is and that I will stand beside her again one day.